AF576772

THE LAST PARADISE

NORTH KOREA

by Nicolas Righetti

TEXT AND PHOTOGRAPHS BY
NICOLAS RIGHETTI
INTRODUCTION BY ORVILLE SCHELL

" The Last Paradise "

ORVILLE SCHELL

For the elect who have managed to gain entrance into the hermetic Democratic People's Republic of Korea (a.k.a. North Korea), a very special feeling of fraternity lingers long after departure from Pyongyang's eerily people-less and silent airport. What unites us in solidarity is a paradox. While we know that we have been to one of the few remaining places in the world that is truly different, we also know that we have all had exactly the same experience: we have been chaperoned by the same official guides or "handlers," stayed at the same two or three hotels, gone to the same performances, visited the same "resort," and trooped through the same revolutionary shrines.

Those who have made this utterly unique East Asian *hajj* have all had the same disorienting, almost out-of-body, experience of transmigrating from our ever more homogenized, quotidian lives in our increasingly globalized world and into this utterly fantastic latter-day Fabergé egg designed in socialist kitsch rather than Czarist baroque. And, after a few days in "the last paradise," we have all experienced a feeling of confusing disap-pointment over the fact that no matter how hard we have tried to elude our handlers in order to catch a glimpse of "the real" North Korea, we have all inevitably failed. And so, upon completing our tours, most of us have left with a sensation of having been somehow cheated—of having been to a place that was so managed that its true reality remained almost completely unrevealed to us.

Indeed, in my experience, returning Pyongyang pilgrims are almost invariably left feeling even a little embarrassed by their inability to get to the heart of the North Korean matter. It takes a while to realize that what we have experienced is something quite other than what we were probably seeking. We have been afforded a virtual adventure outside of the cyber world. We have had an experience akin to visiting a faraway museum where we are able to commune with a series of carefully constructed dioramas based not on life during some past historical period, but on a far more fantastical world: what Korean life could be like—should be like—if only the Great Leader Kim Il Sung and his son, the Dear Leader Kim Jong Il, could make their word "the ideology of Juche" flesh.

The metaphor of a museum is doubly apt in North Korea's case, because what a foreign visitor has the chance to observe is the last remaining example of those once myriad Marxist-Leninist revolutions that once swept the globe, promising their downtrodden peoples a "socialist paradise." Now, however, like the wooly mammoth or the flightless auk, these revolutions, too, have all but vanished into political extinction.

Having closely observed other socialist movements and their big leader kulturs—such as that of Mao Zedong, Ho Chi-minh, and Pol Pot—during the high tide of their most extreme Communist pretensions, and having watched them implode before anyone could properly chronicle or photograph their revolutions, one feels an undeniable urgency to catch what must inevitably be the waning days of this last example of heroic Stalinist revolution. As the twenty-first century begins, what is wanted is for someone to freeze-frame in amber this fabulous North Korean hallucination of the future, to preserve it for posterity before it, too, evanesces irremediably into the past.

This is what Swiss photographer Nicolas Righetti has done. Without lamenting his inability to get under the skin of this evasive, Potemkin-ized land, he has instead decided to embrace the illusory surface of what North Korean officials want a visitor to see, thereby allowing us to share their leaders' fantasy of their own revolution. By visually capturing the overblown, chimerical vision of North Korean socialism so that we can begin to make sense of it, Righetti does for us something akin to what Freudian psychoanalysts do for their individual analysands when they help them recapture the vividness of a dream, the better to plum their psychological psychosis. By doing so, Righetti helps highlight the pathological yearnings that the leaders of this brutal and failed state have to maintain a heroic and triumphant pose even as their magnificently mad revolutionary quest fails.

The Last Paradise is an important work, because as we approach the last chapter of the twentieth century's enthrallment with the tectonic and savage forces of "socialist revolution," it is critical that we remember just how hysterically disassociated the larger-than-life and utterly undemocratic leaders who led these movements became from the very world of which they proclaimed themselves the saviors.

In this sense, the seeming unreality of North Korea's revolutionary "paradise" is, in fact, profoundly telling. It reminds us how grand pretensions all too often lead to monumental failure, and how, in turn, such failure leads to a devastating sense of loss of face and thus desperate efforts to construct an utterly fanciful parallel, or alternative, reality as a form of compensation for the yawning abyss of their failure. It is the stubborn insistence on maintaining the semblance of this fanciful, virtual world of revolutionary accomplishment, where none exists in reality, that makes North Korea such an interesting and important place to visit.

It is, of course, undeniably true that if you journey to North Korea, you will see nothing of the "real life" of this benighted land; namely, no starving peasants, no nuclear weapons sites, and no political prisons.

Indeed, you will see nothing except what the government and Workers' Party want you to see. But through these carefully managed tours, one is able to experience something of the disembodied stage-set of what this socialist dream was supposed to look like when it was finally and fully fledged through revolutionary action. And this is something truly worth seeing and reflecting on, lest the next time purveyors of political utopias come plying their grand visions, and a large portion of the world once again surrenders to their artful seduction.

" In North Korea,
many forms of art flourish
in people's lives, to the extent
that it would not be an exaggeration
to say that the country itself
is a work of art. "

NADA TAKASHI, JAPANESE JOURNALIST

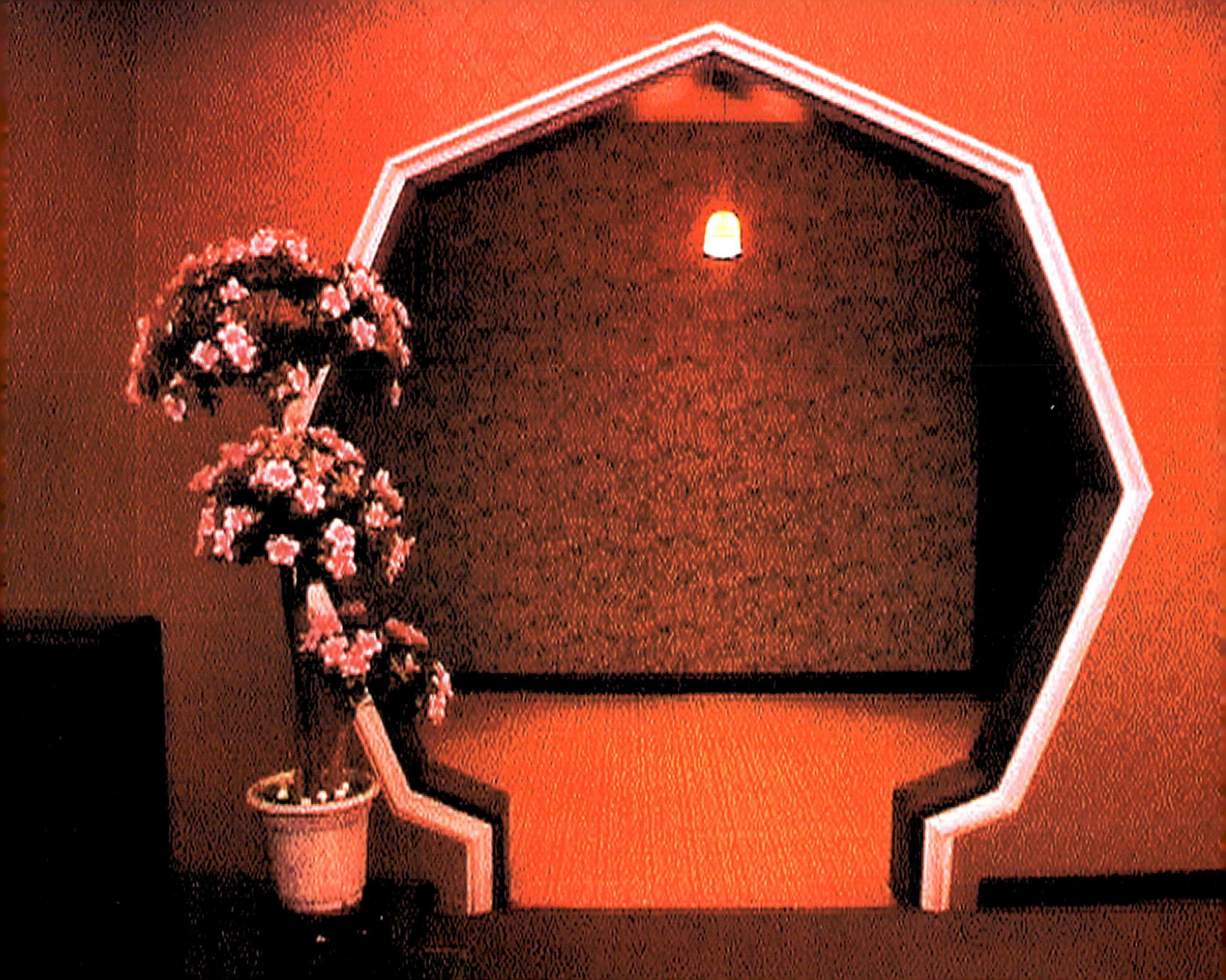

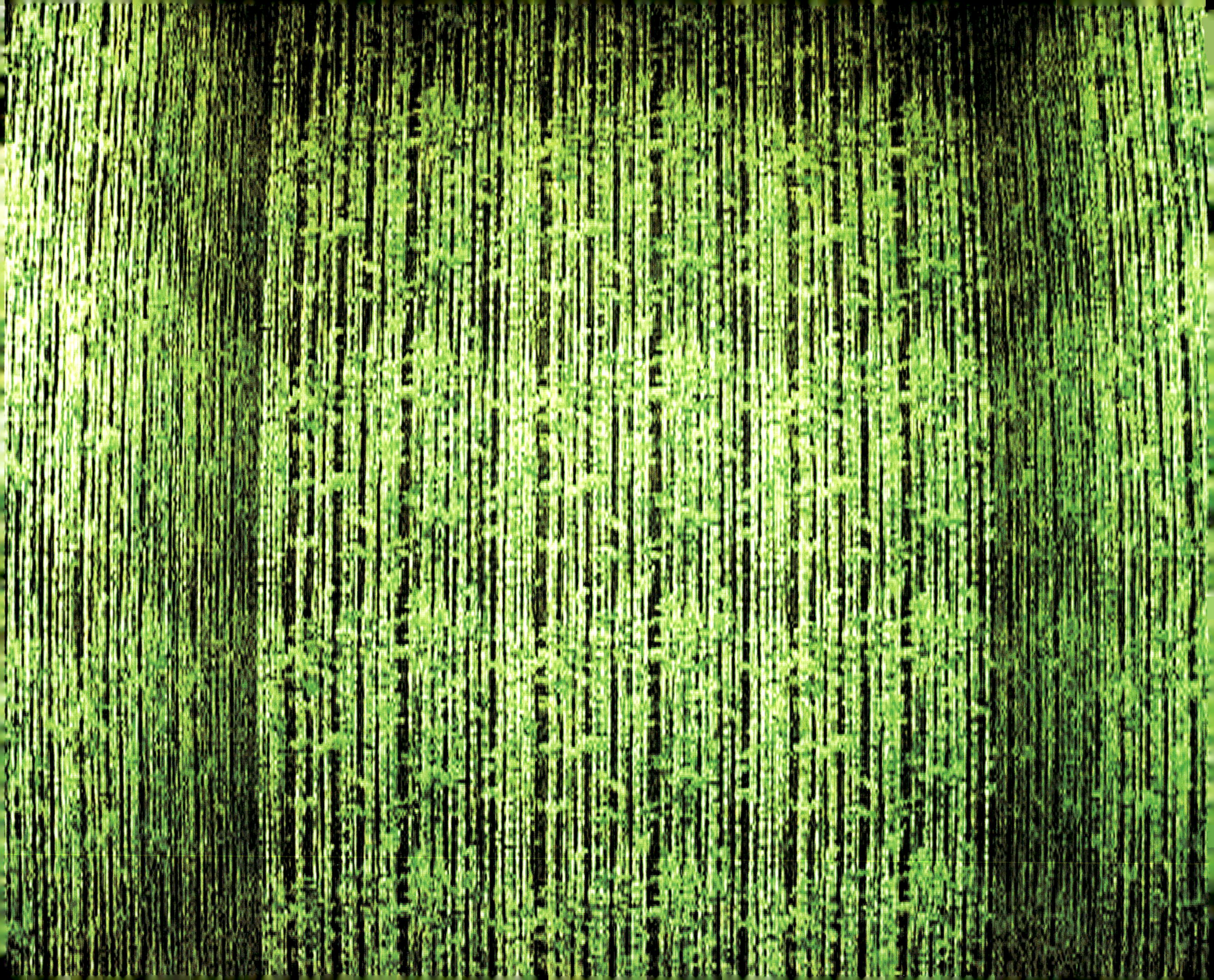

YEAR ZERO (1911) **The start of Juche calendar. Adopted in 1995, the new calendar begins the year Kim Il Sung was conceived.**

" We are in Paradise. "

SLOGAN IN THE STREETS OF PYONGYANG

YEAR 1 (APRIL 15, 1912) **Kim Il Sung is born as Kim Song Ju in Mangyongdae, near Pyongyang. Kim Il Sung was born during a time of colonization and repression of Korean culture by the Japanese. Japan had annexed Korea in 1910, replacing the Korean Emperor with a Japanese "resident-general." Japanese culture, language, and religion were imposed on the Korean people. In 1925 Kim's family flees to Manchuria to escape the Japanese occupation. As a teenager, Kim joins the communist party, changes name to Kim Il Sung, and joins the resistance against the Japanese.**

President Kim Il Sung received this gun from
father. The Supreme Leader used this gun

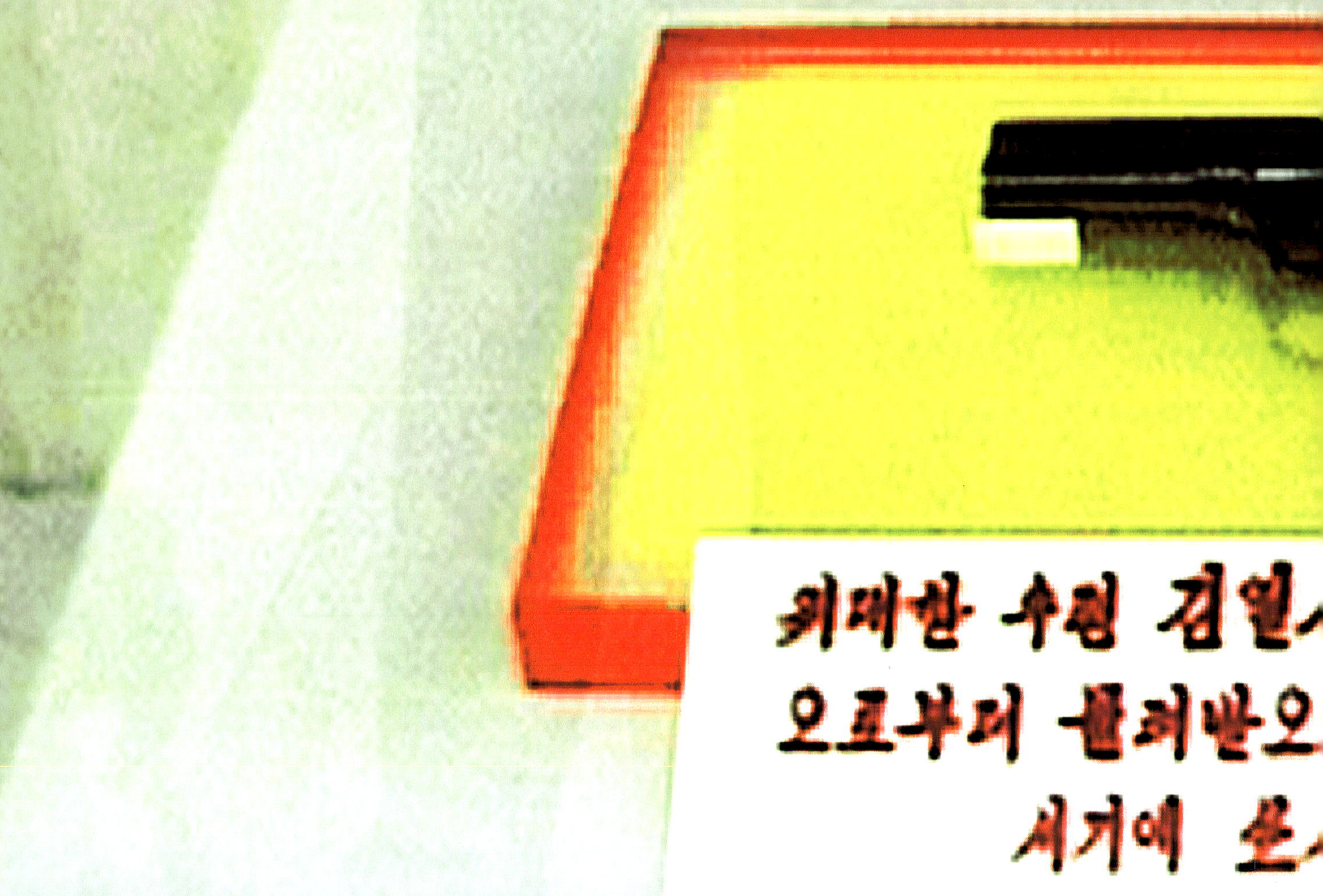

his mother—it originally belonged to his
to launch armed combat. WALL LABEL, WAR MUSEUM

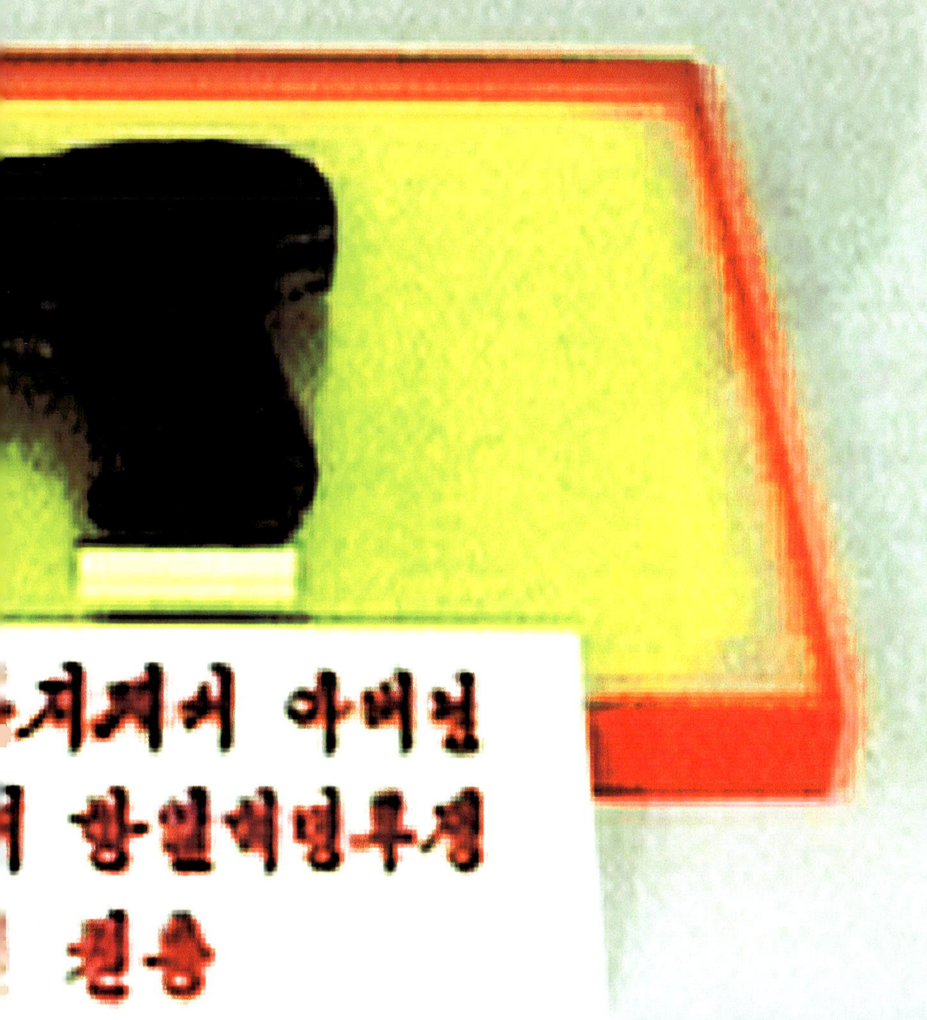

"The decor reflects the era."

KIM JONG IL

YEAR 31 (FEBURARY 11, 1942) **Kim Jong Il, the son of Kim Il Sung, is born in the Soviet Union, although official party line holds that he was born at the foot of the sacred Mount Paektu in North Korea.**

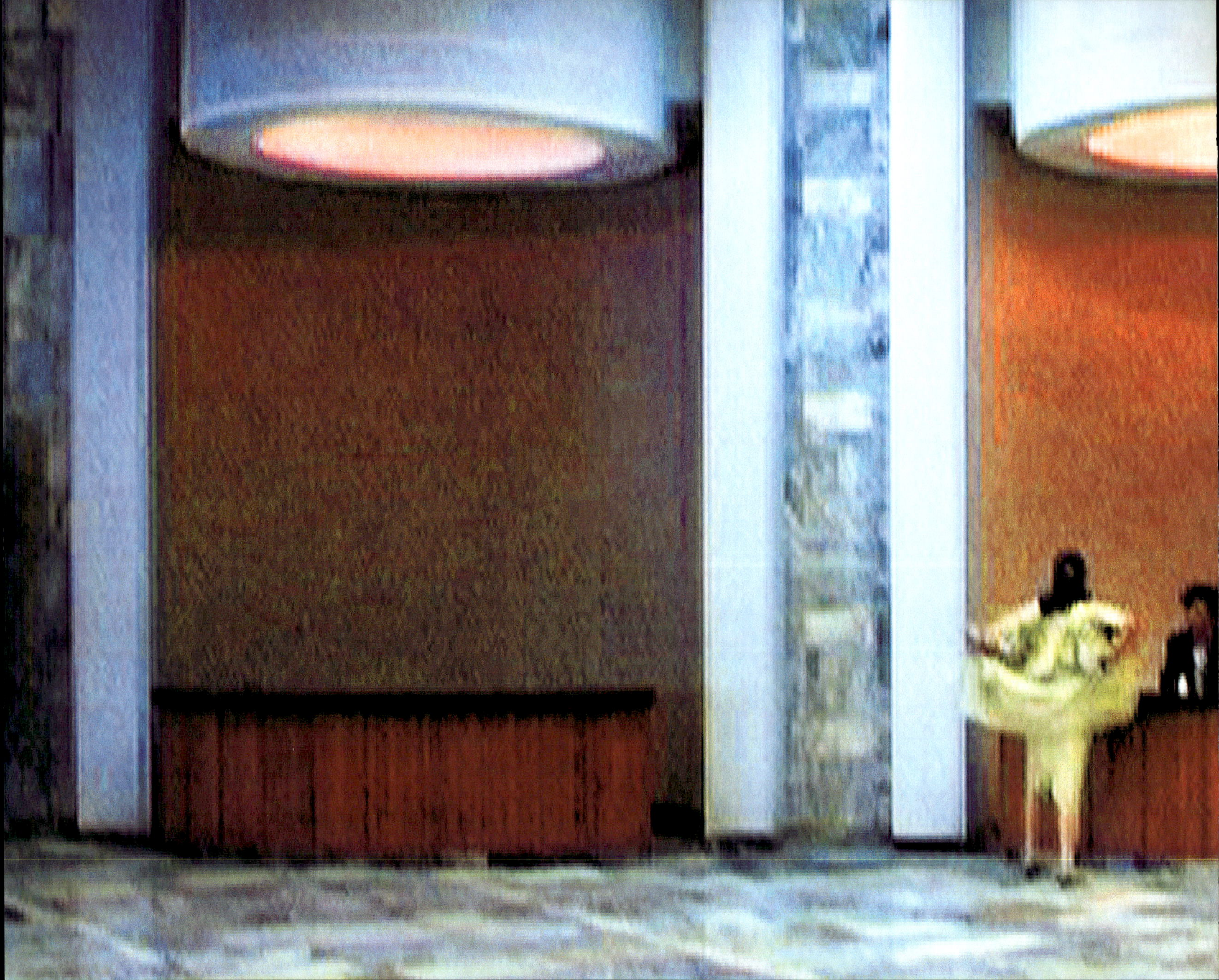

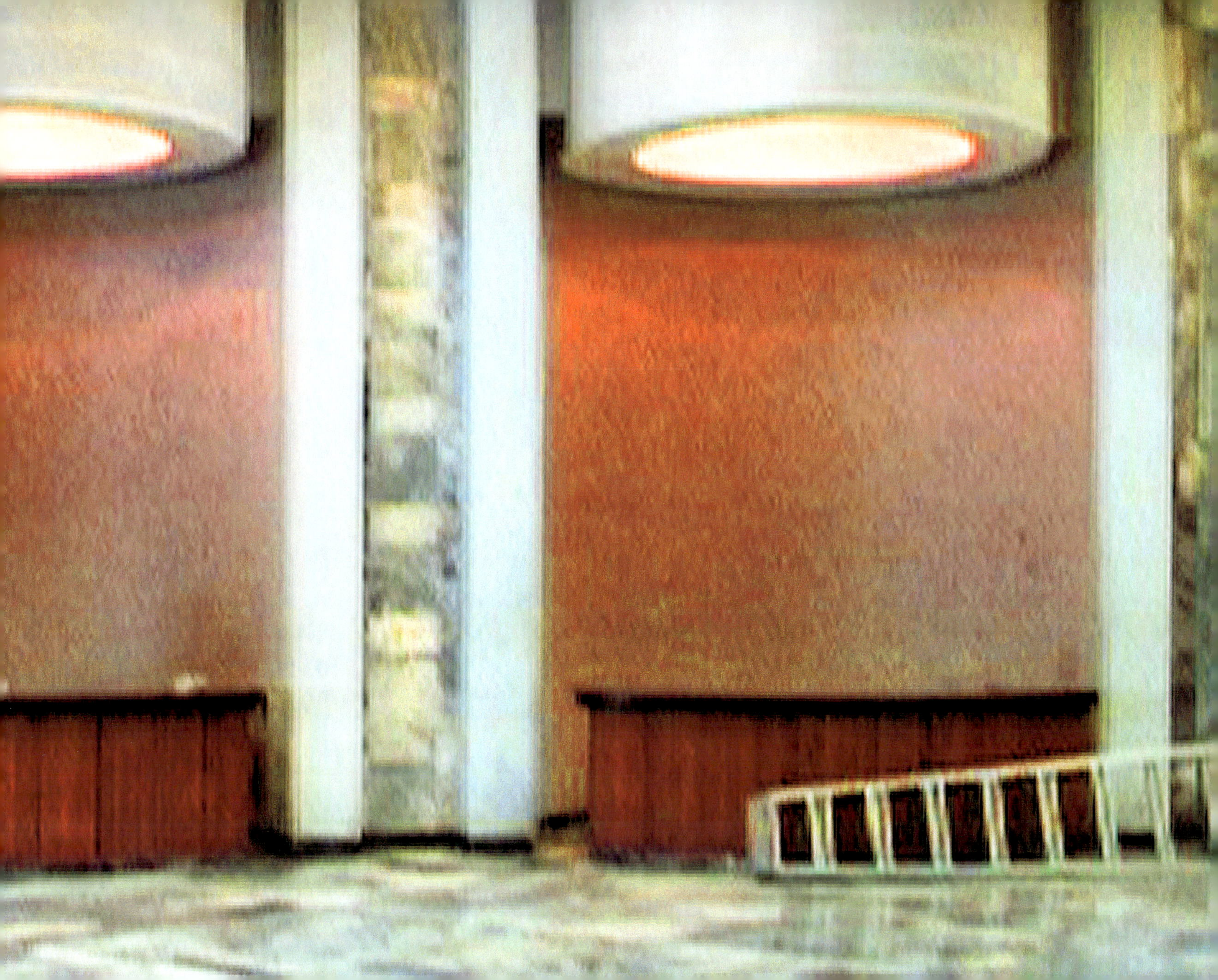

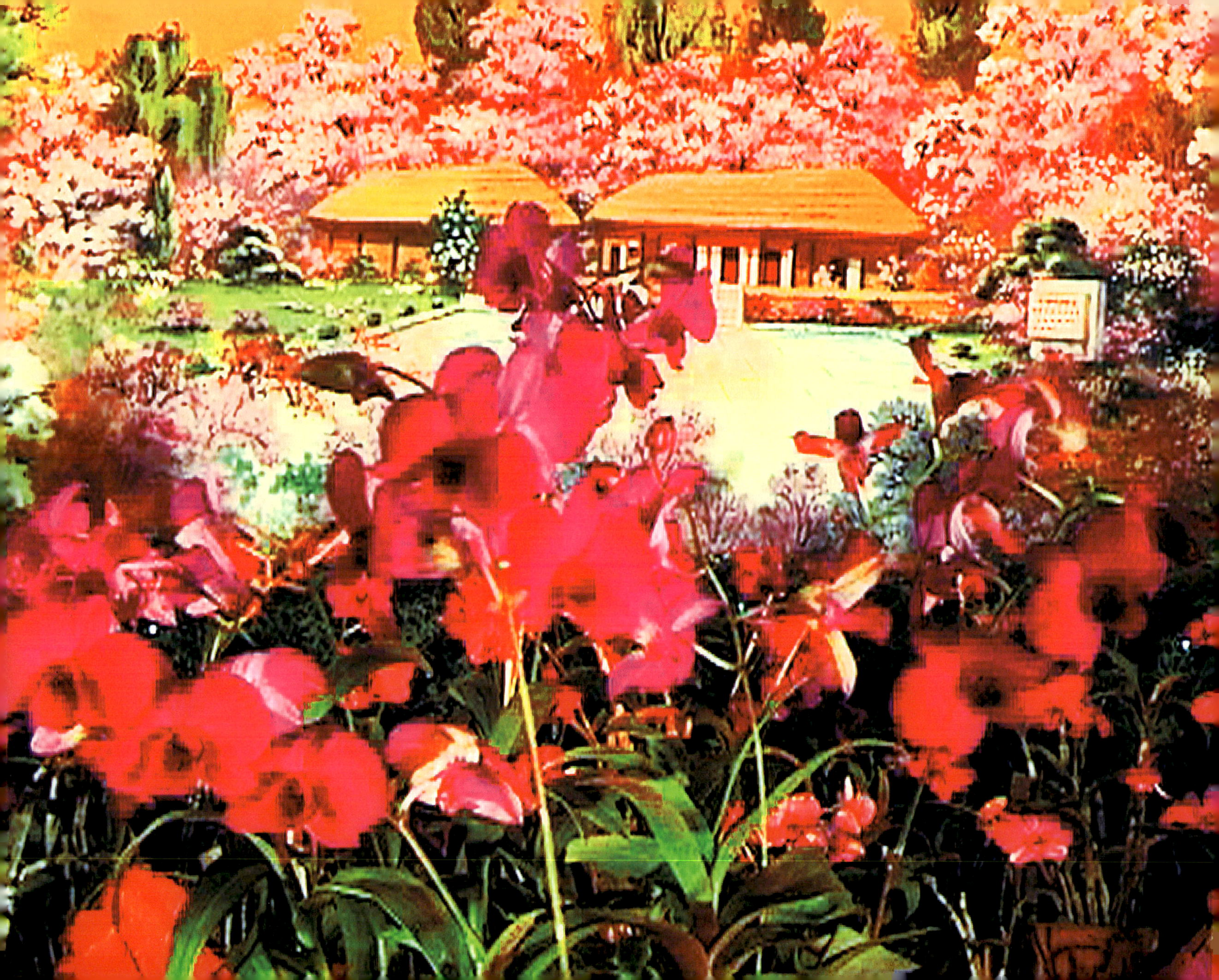

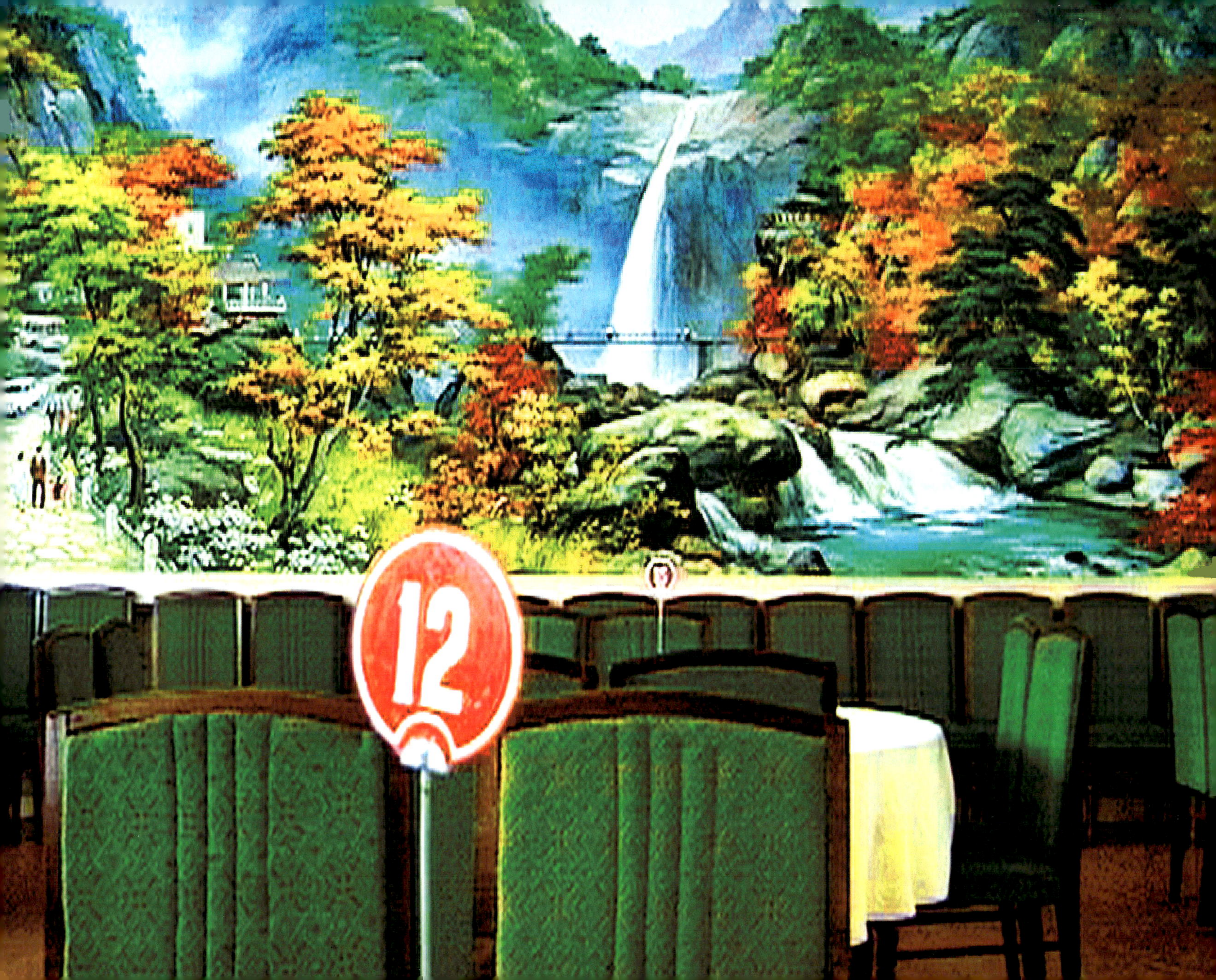
12

"The revolutionary pool"

OFFICIAL GUIDE, HAN KIL HO

YEAR 34 (SEPTEMBER 2, 1945) **The 38th Parallel is chosen by the U.S. War Department as the dividing line between the U.S. and the U.S.S.R: Americans are to accept the surrender of the Japanese army in the South, and the Soviets are to accept the surrender of troops in the North. It is intended as a temporary solution, but with Soviet and American troops occupying each sphere, the division of territories quickly becomes solidified by the politics of the Cold War.**

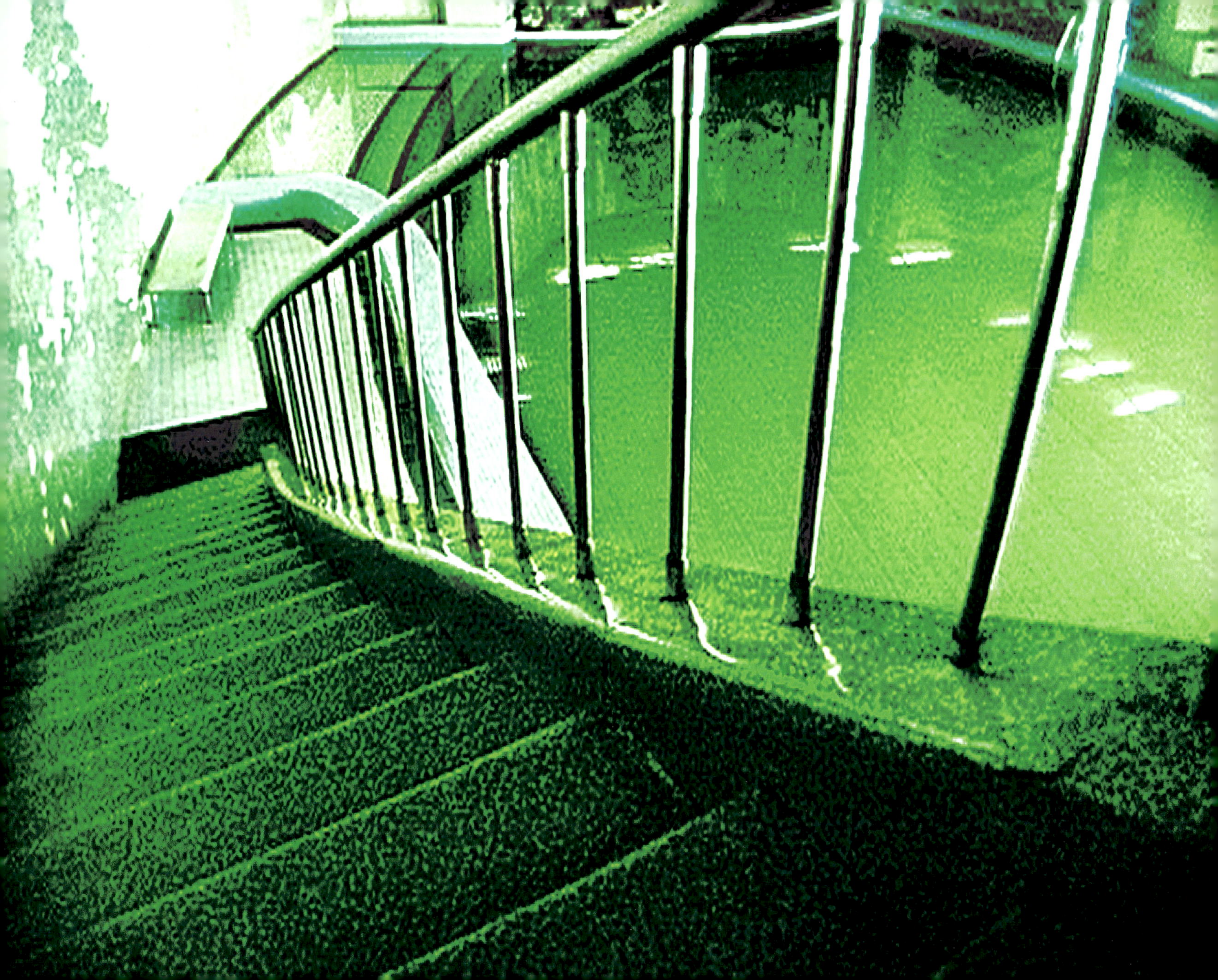

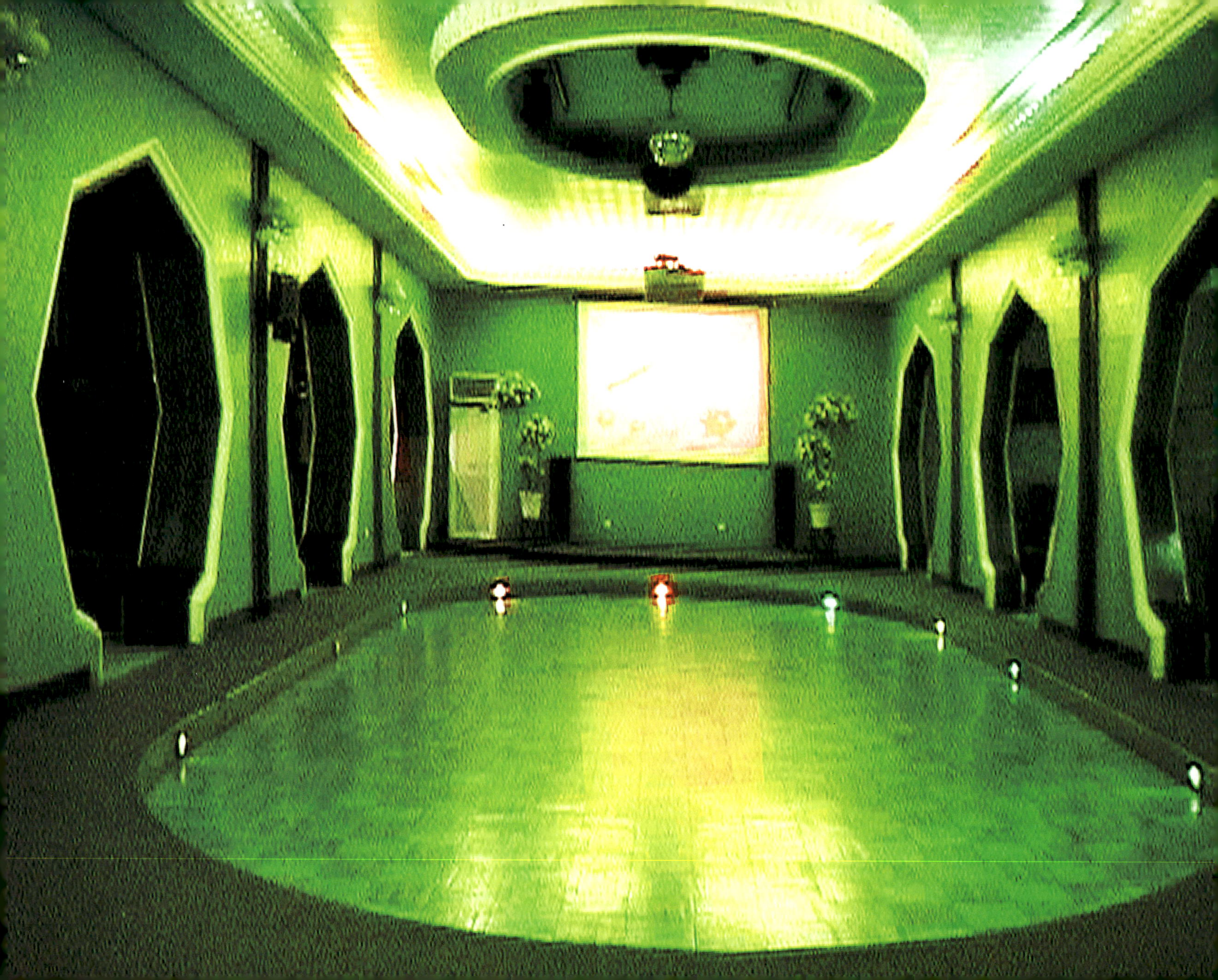

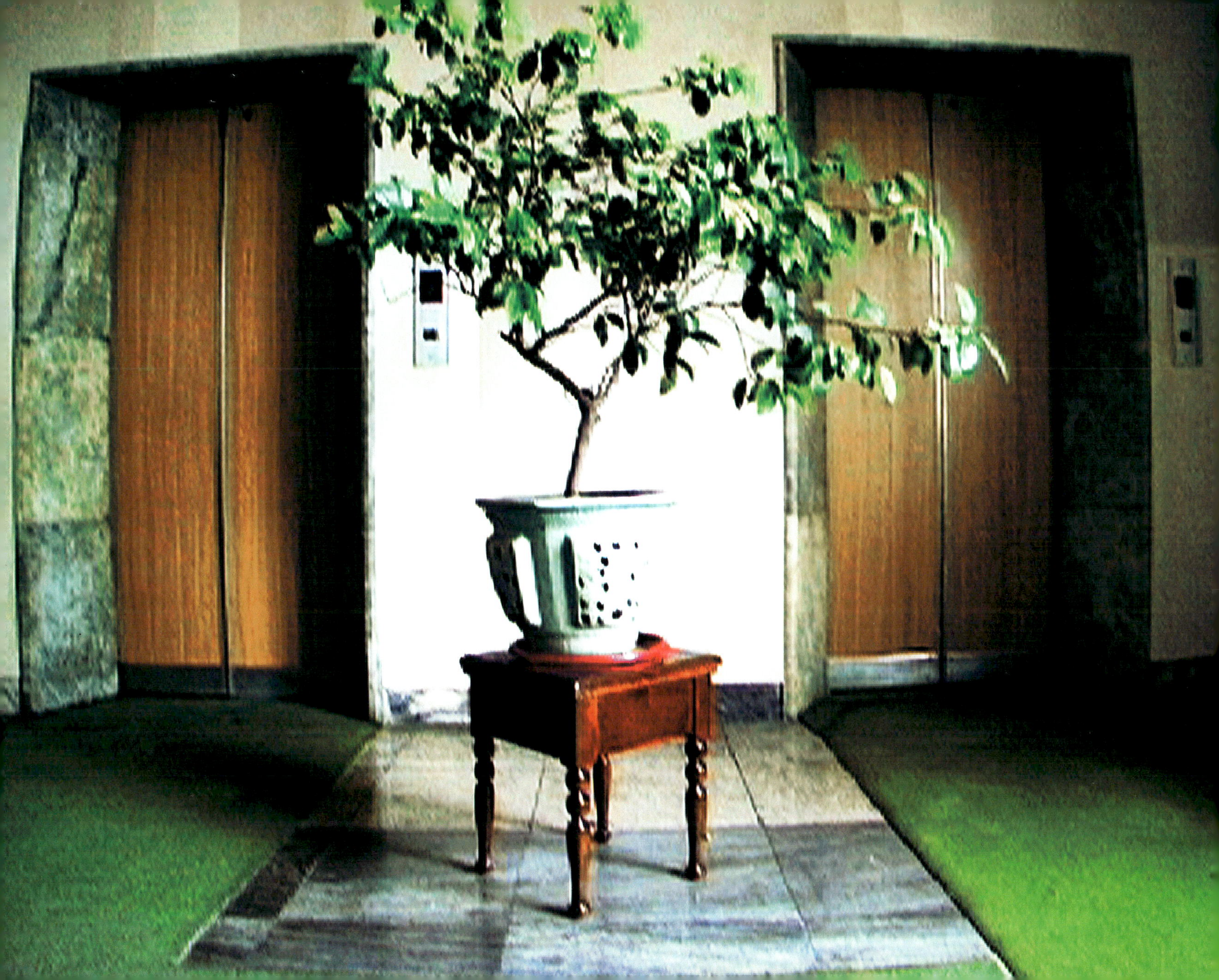

" Kim Il Sung, you have a dazzling smile! "

NEWS FROM PYONGYANG

YEAR 34 (OCTOBER 9, 1945) **Kim Il Sung, now a major in the Soviet army, returns to Korea from Siberia and is given accolades as a heroic leader of the resistance against the Japanese. He organizes the Workers' Party of Korea and quickly rises to leadership position as the head of the Interim People's Committee.** YEAR 37 (SEPTEMBER 9, 1948) **American-supported Syngman Rhee is selected by the National Assembly to become the first President of the Republic of Korea in the south. A month later, Soviet-backed Kim Il Sung is named premier of the newly named Democratic People's Republic of Korea.**

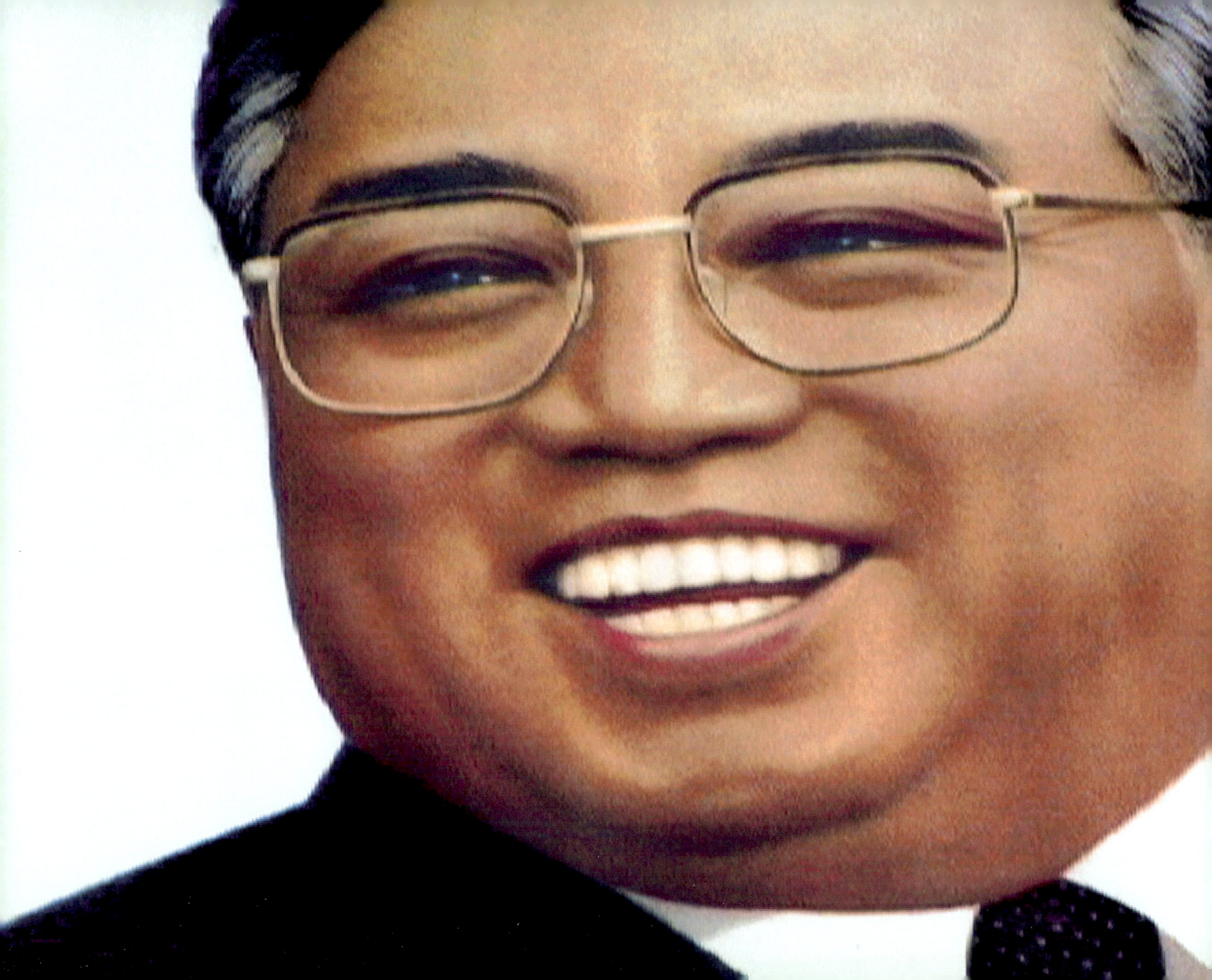

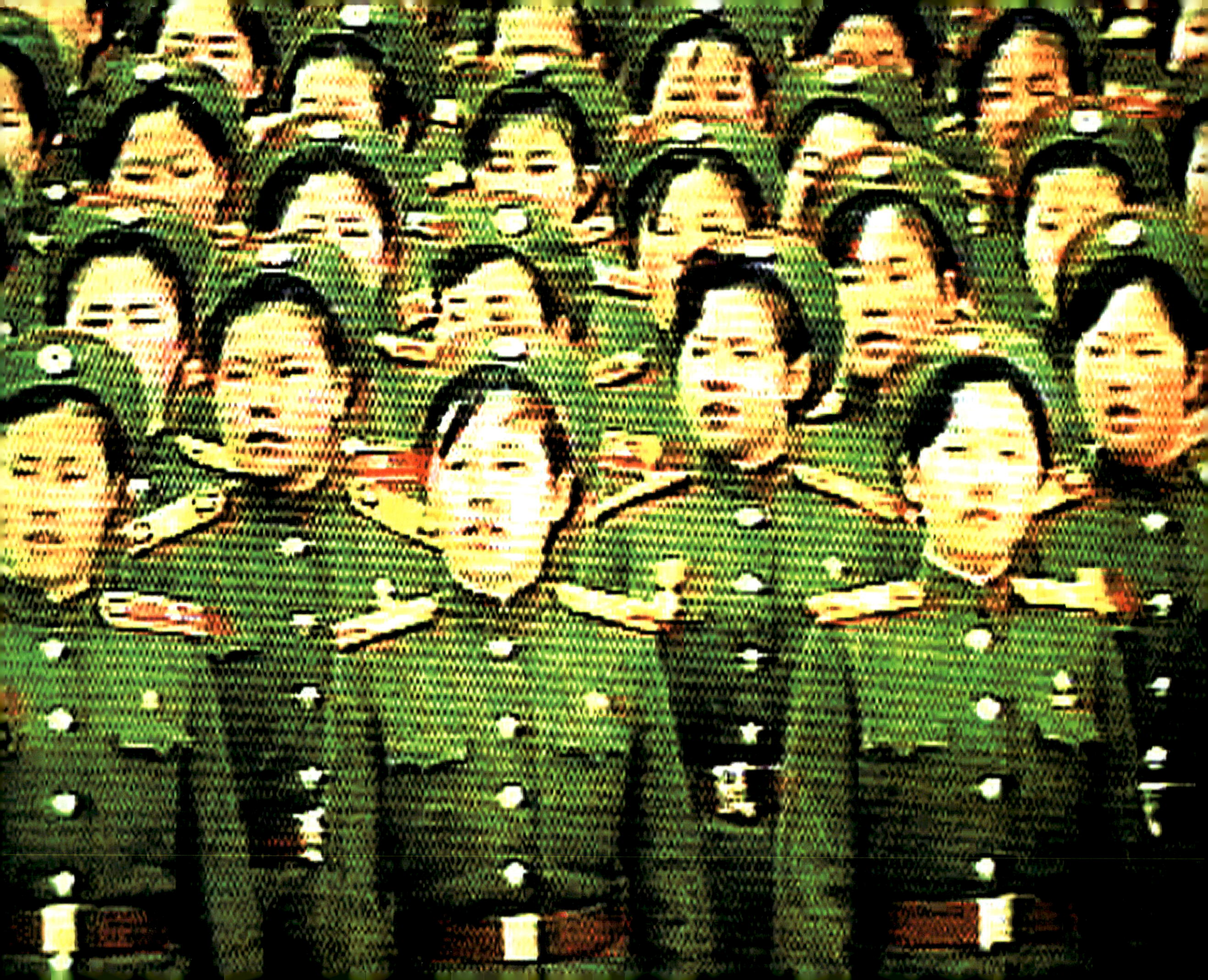

"The people are my God."

KIM IL SUNG

YEAR 39 (JUNE 25, 1950) **With Stalin's approval, Kim Il Sung sends troops across the 38th parallel in an attempt to forcefully unify Korea under his power. Southern forces collapse and the UN intervenes in the war under American military command, pushing the North back. The involvement of the United States triggers a further response by China; Mao sends "the Chinese People's Volunteer Army" to fight with the North against South Korea and the U.S.**

" A soldier has to be prepared to defend his leader with his life, to the extent of being a human bomb."

KIM JONG IL

YEAR 40 (JANUARY – MAY 1951) **In the course of five months, Seoul changes hands three times between the communist forces of North Korea and China and the United Nations-backed forces consisting primarily of U.S. and South Korean troops. By May, the North Korean forces are finally and definitively pushed back.**

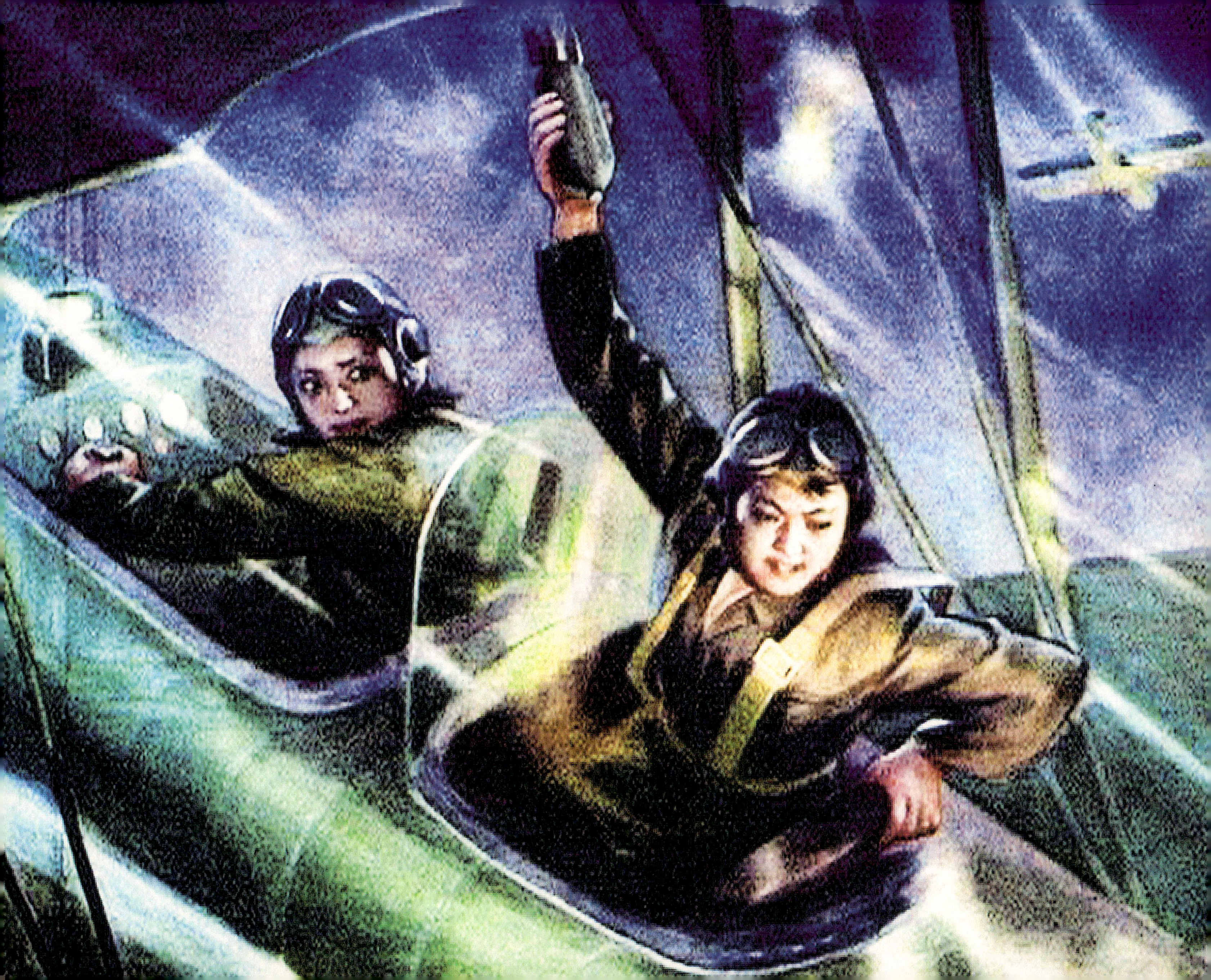

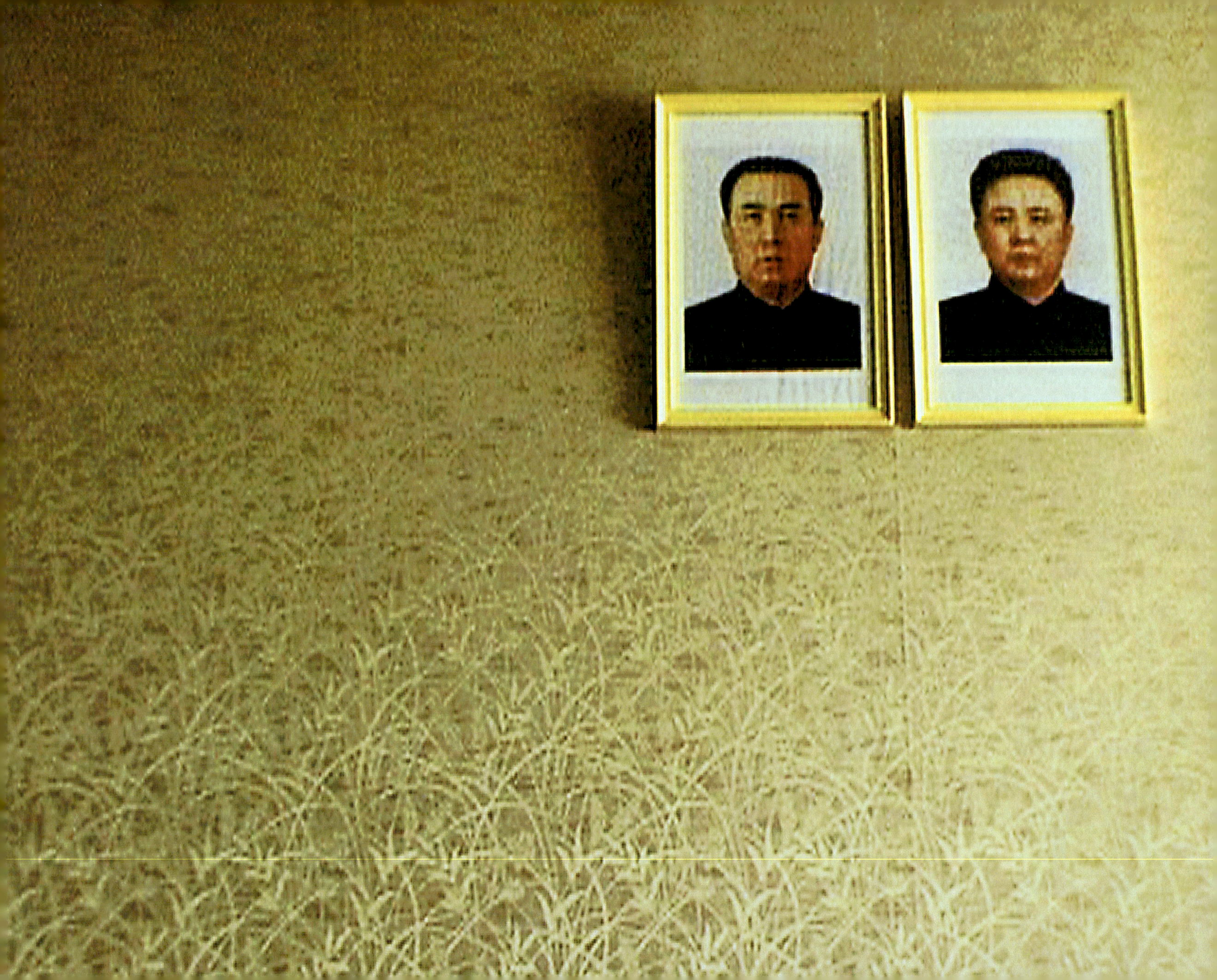

"An iron discipline must prevail in our earthly paradise."

NEWS FROM PYONGYANG

YEAR 42 (JULY 27, 1953) **North Korea signs an armistice agreement with the United States, bringing an end to the Korean War and formally establishing the DMZ (demilitarized zone) as the border between the North and the South. Roughly 3 million peaple are dead or missing and the infrastructure of both sides suffer massive damages. Despite the cessation of hostilities, a formal peace treaty was never signed.**

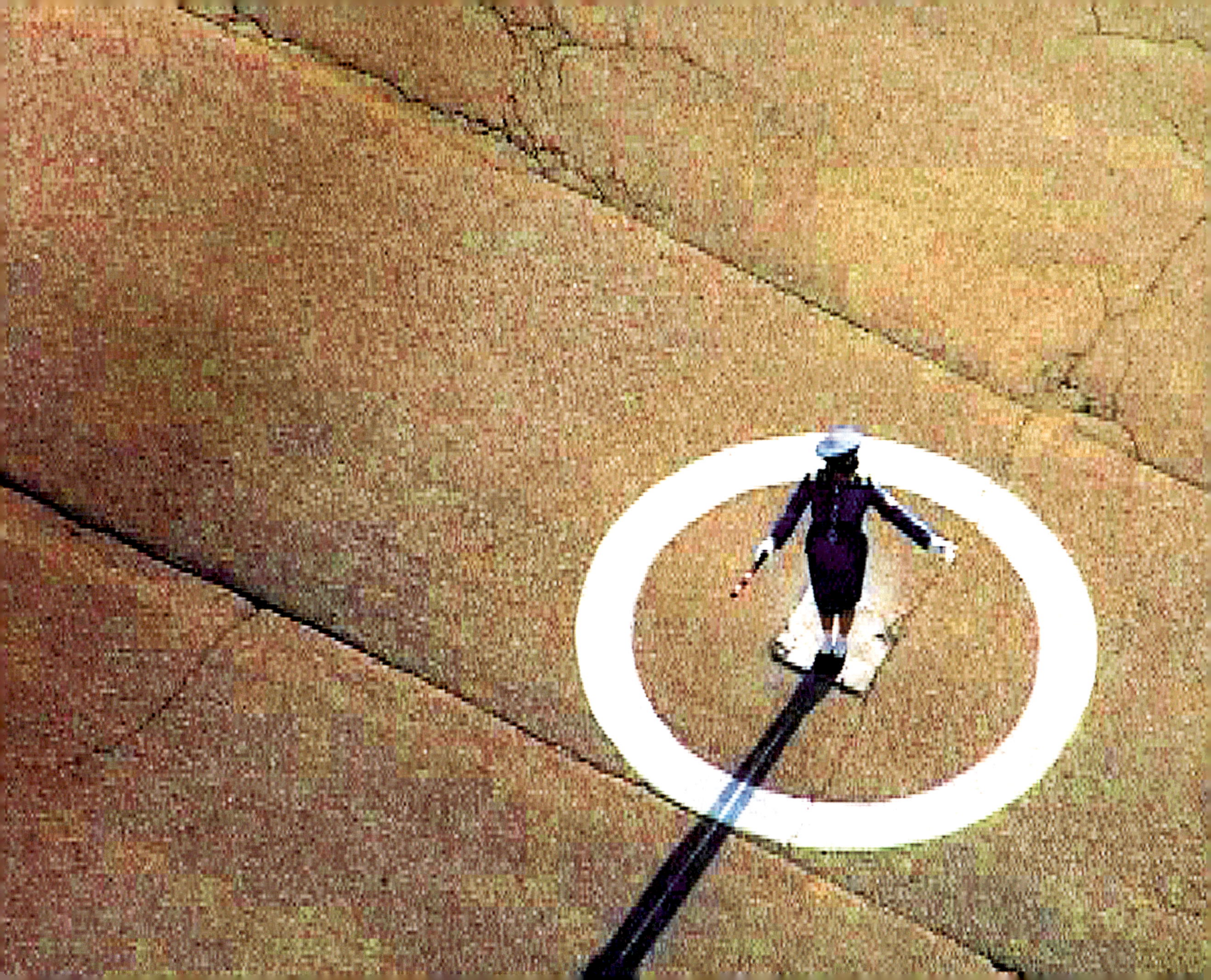

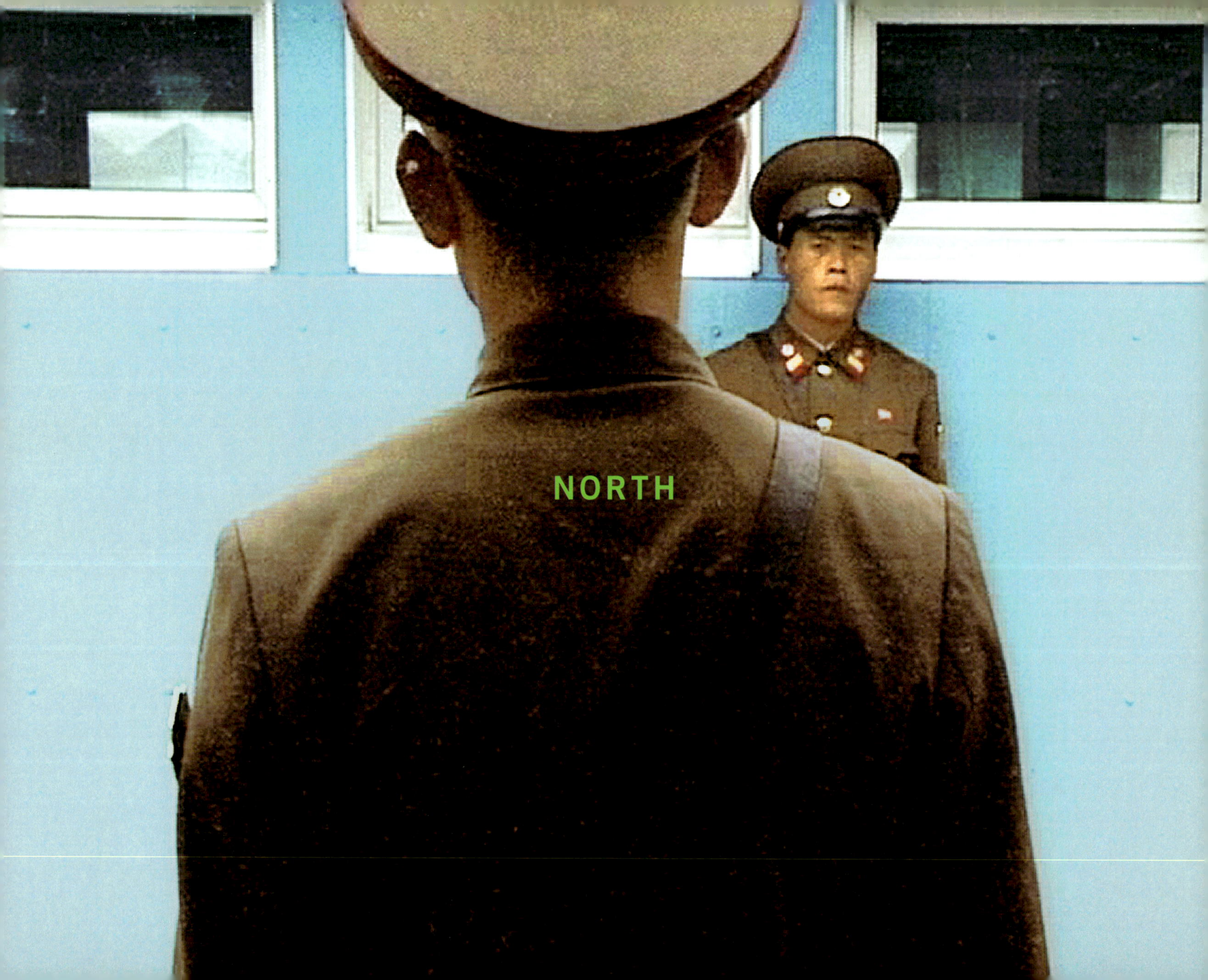

NORTH

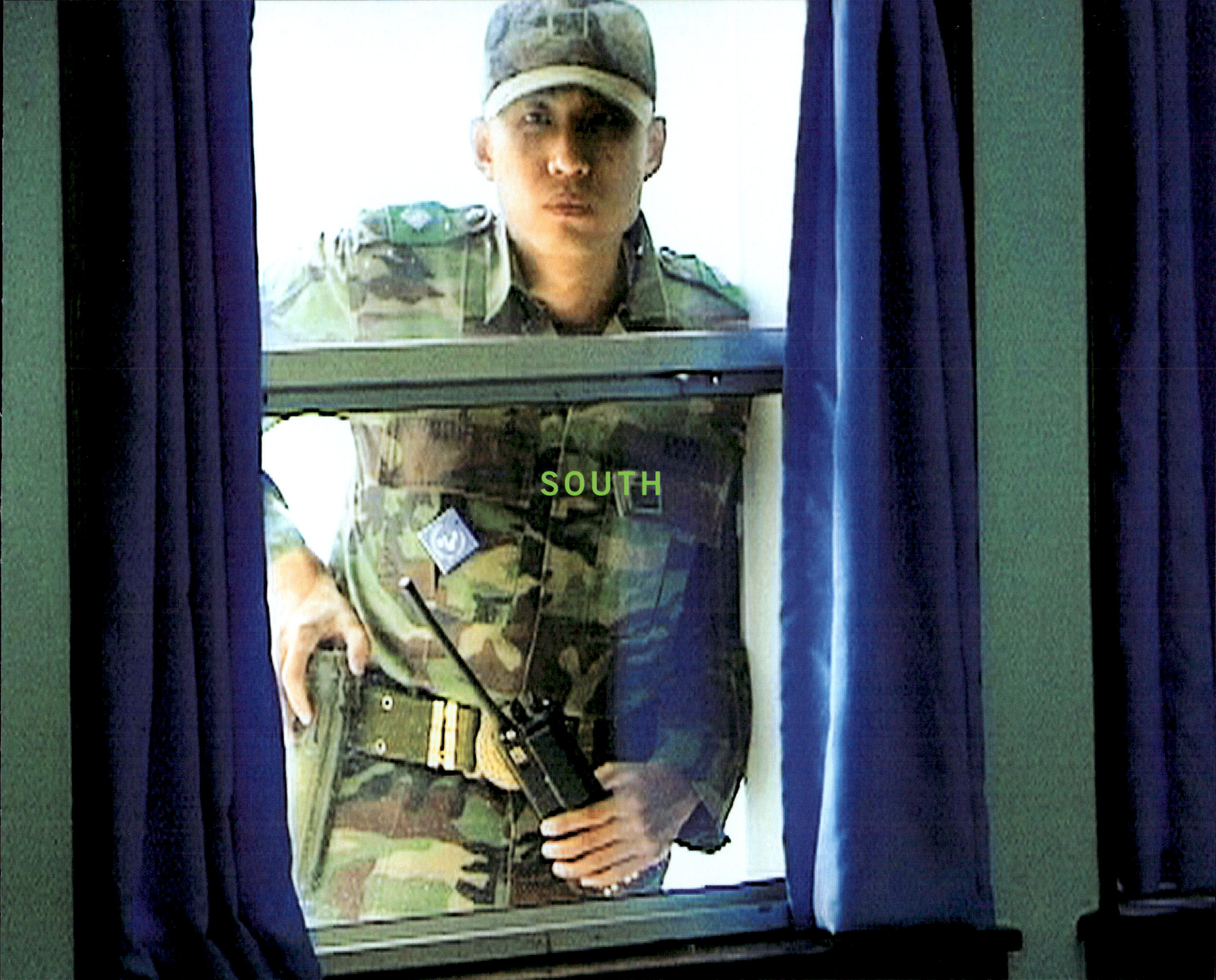
SOUTH

" The State Party takes complete charge
population's living conditions. They
members of society and encourage

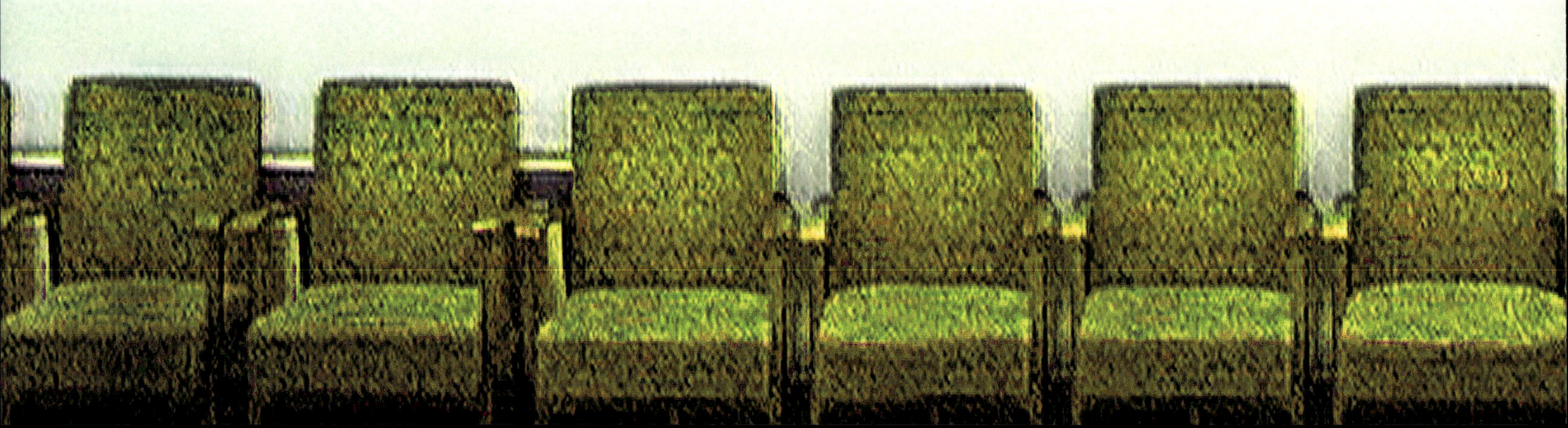

of the country's economy, as well as the endeavour to educate or re-educate all them to join the Party. " PYONGYANG FOREIGN LANGUAGE EDITION

YEAR 42 (AUGUST 3, 1953) **Kim Sung Il consolidates his power, and initiates a series of purges and trials against high-ranking officials in the North Korean party who might oppose him. Any critique or perceived disrespect of the Great Leader is severely quashed.** YEAR 51 (APRIL 15, 1962) **During a banquet, Kim Il Sung congratulates himself on "the execution of all Protestant and Catholic church officials."**

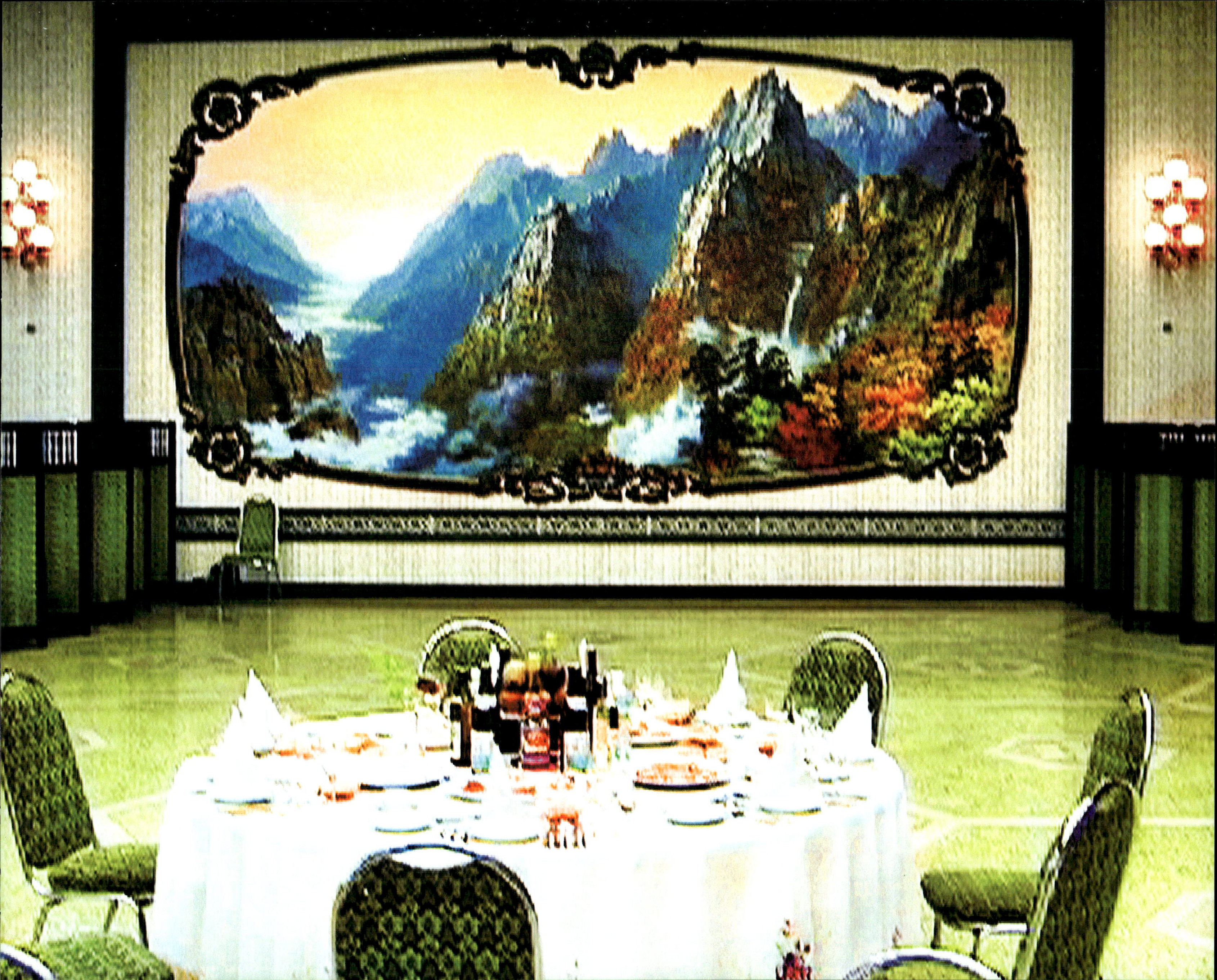

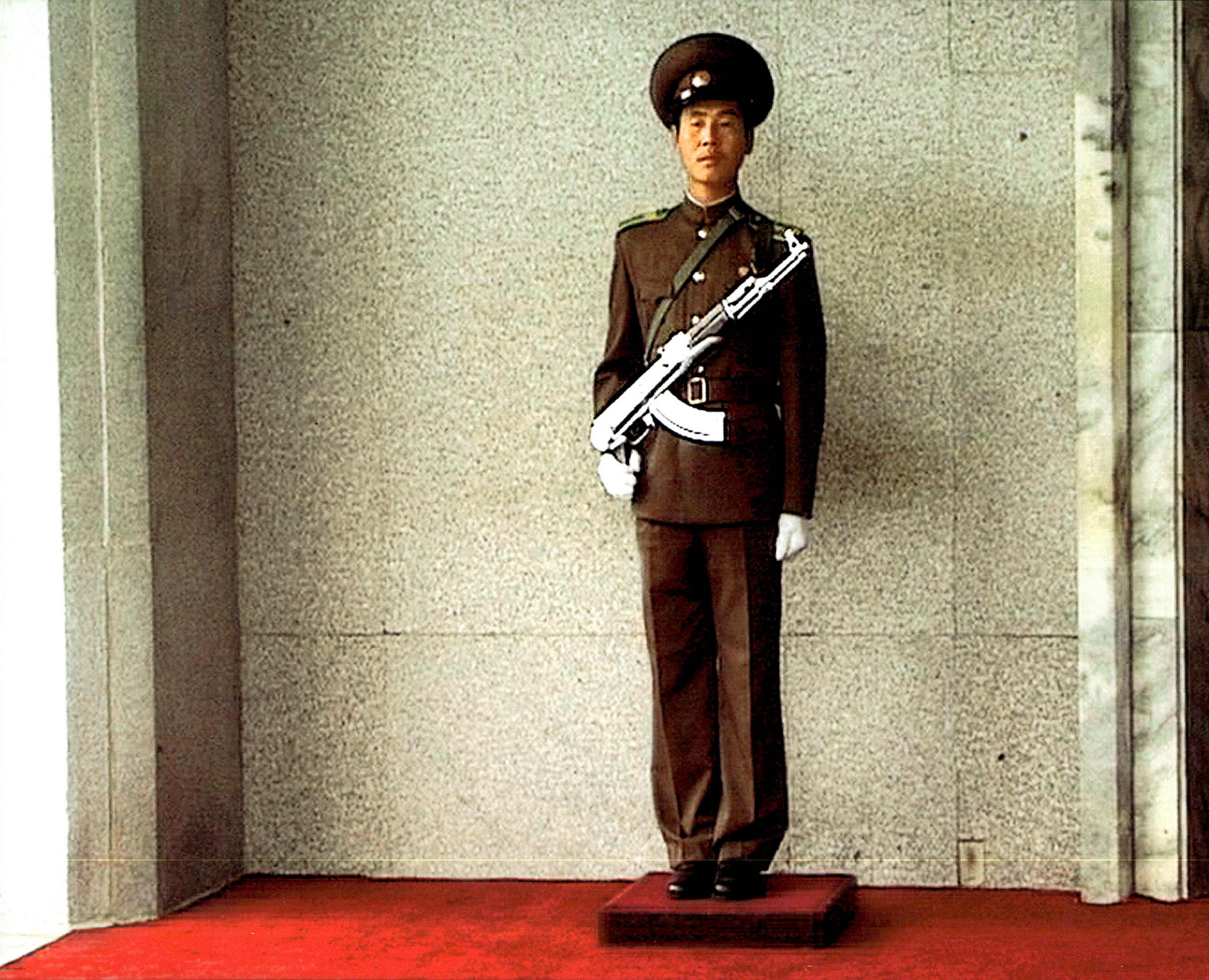

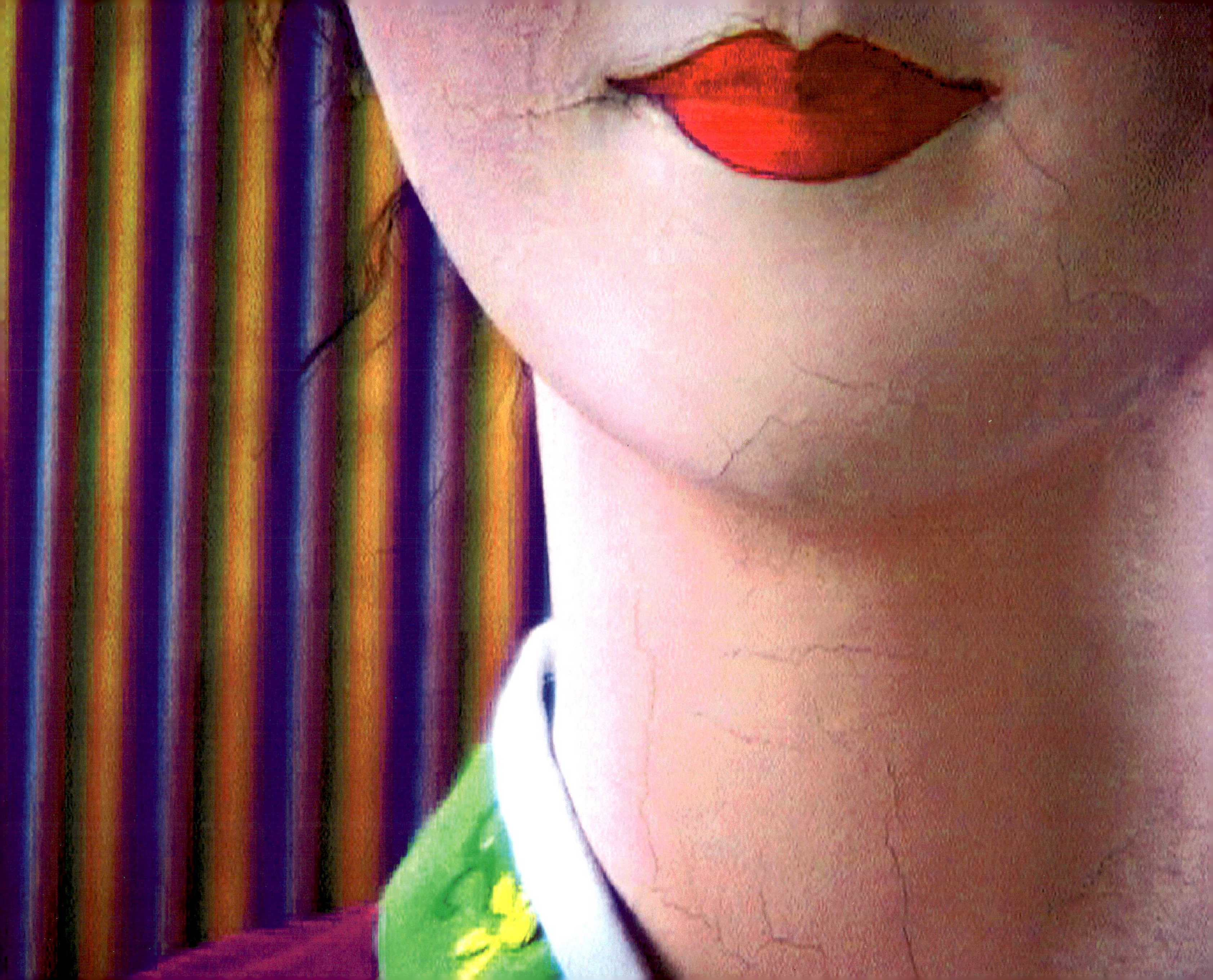

" We have nothing to envy
the rest of the world. "

KIM JONG IL

YEAR 56 (DECEMBER 16, 1967) **Kim Il Sung announces the launch of "Ten Major Independence Platforms" based on ideology of independence, self-reliance, and self-defense, also known as Juche.**

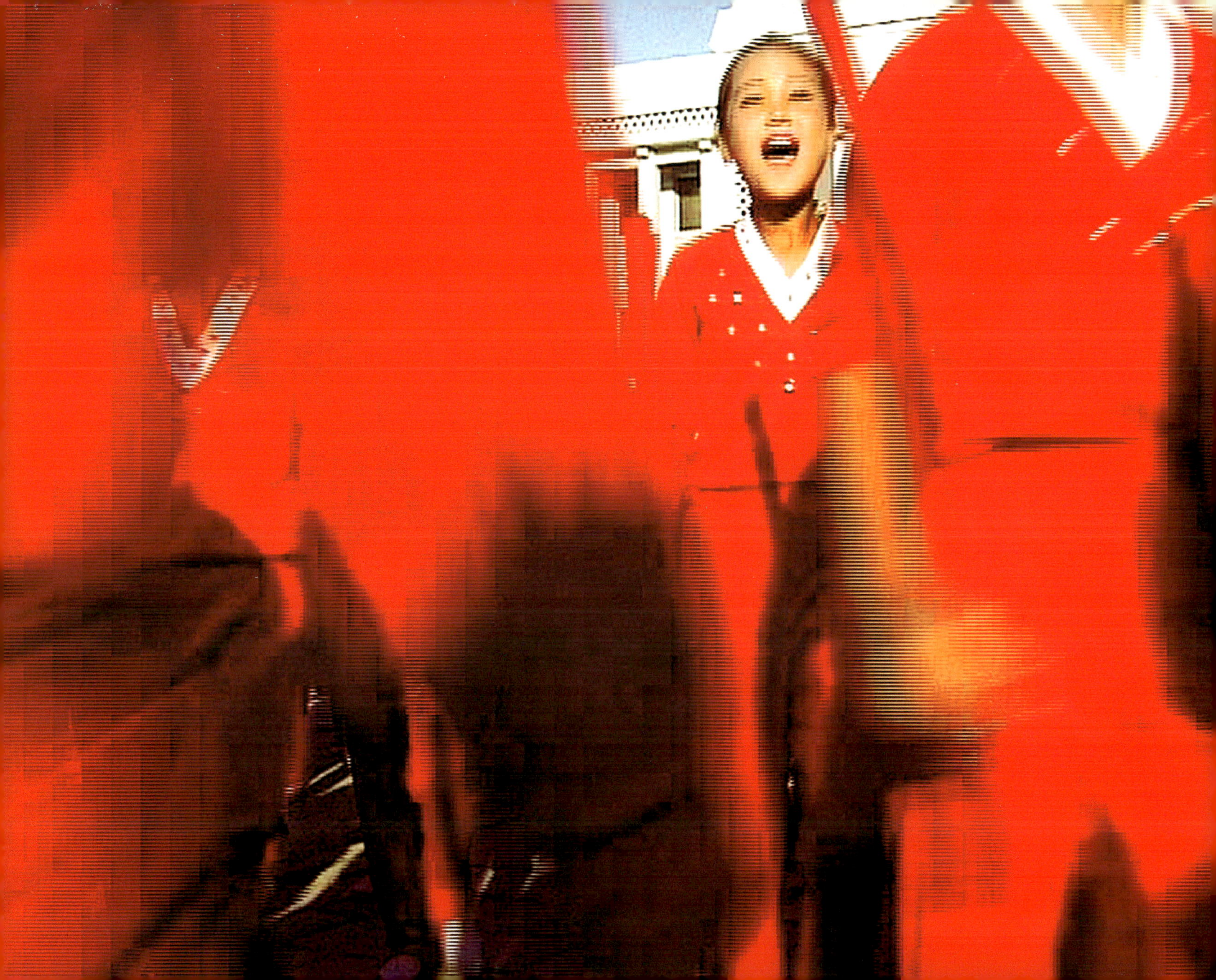

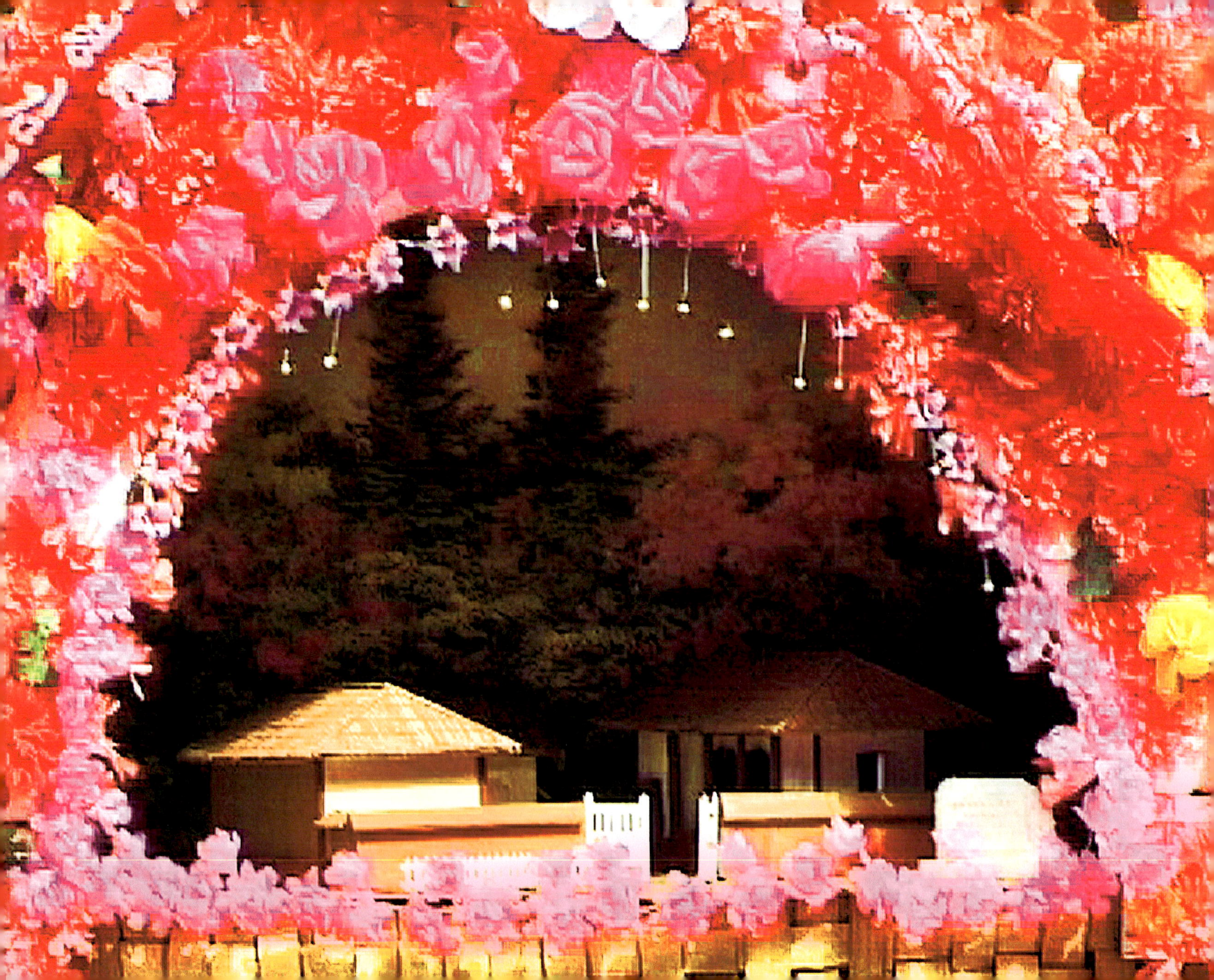

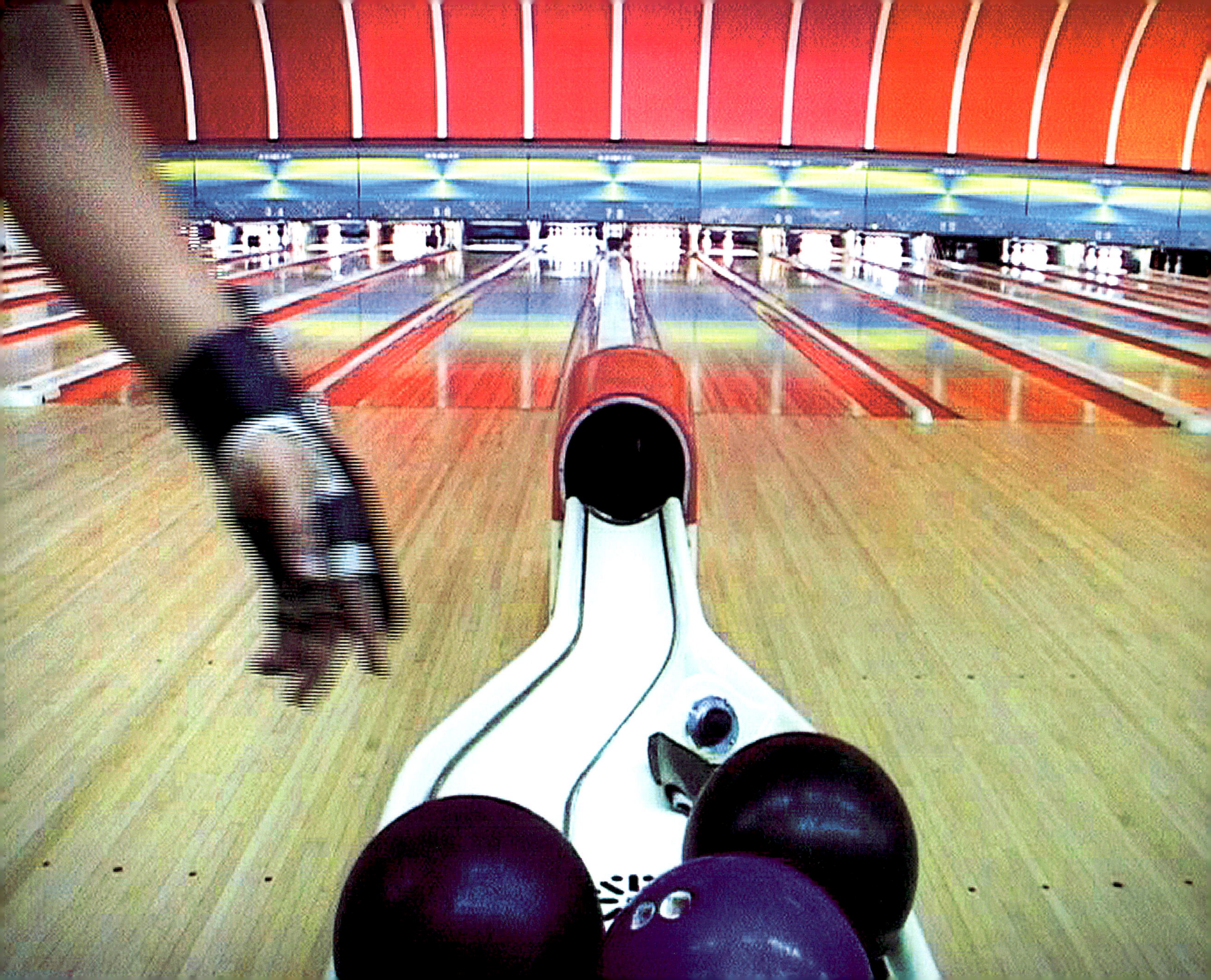

" Art is the party. "

KIM IL SUNG

YEAR 63 (AUGUST 15, 1974) **A North Korean agent attempts to assassinate South Korean President Chung Hee Park, a former general and veteran of the Japanese Imperial Army, who seized power in a military coup. The assassination fails, but the first lady is killed during the attempt.**
YEAR 76 (NOVEMBER 29, 1987) **Under orders to "throw a wrench into the two-Korea policy and preparations for the Olympics," North Korean agents plant a bomb on a Korean Airlines flight, killing all 115 on board.**

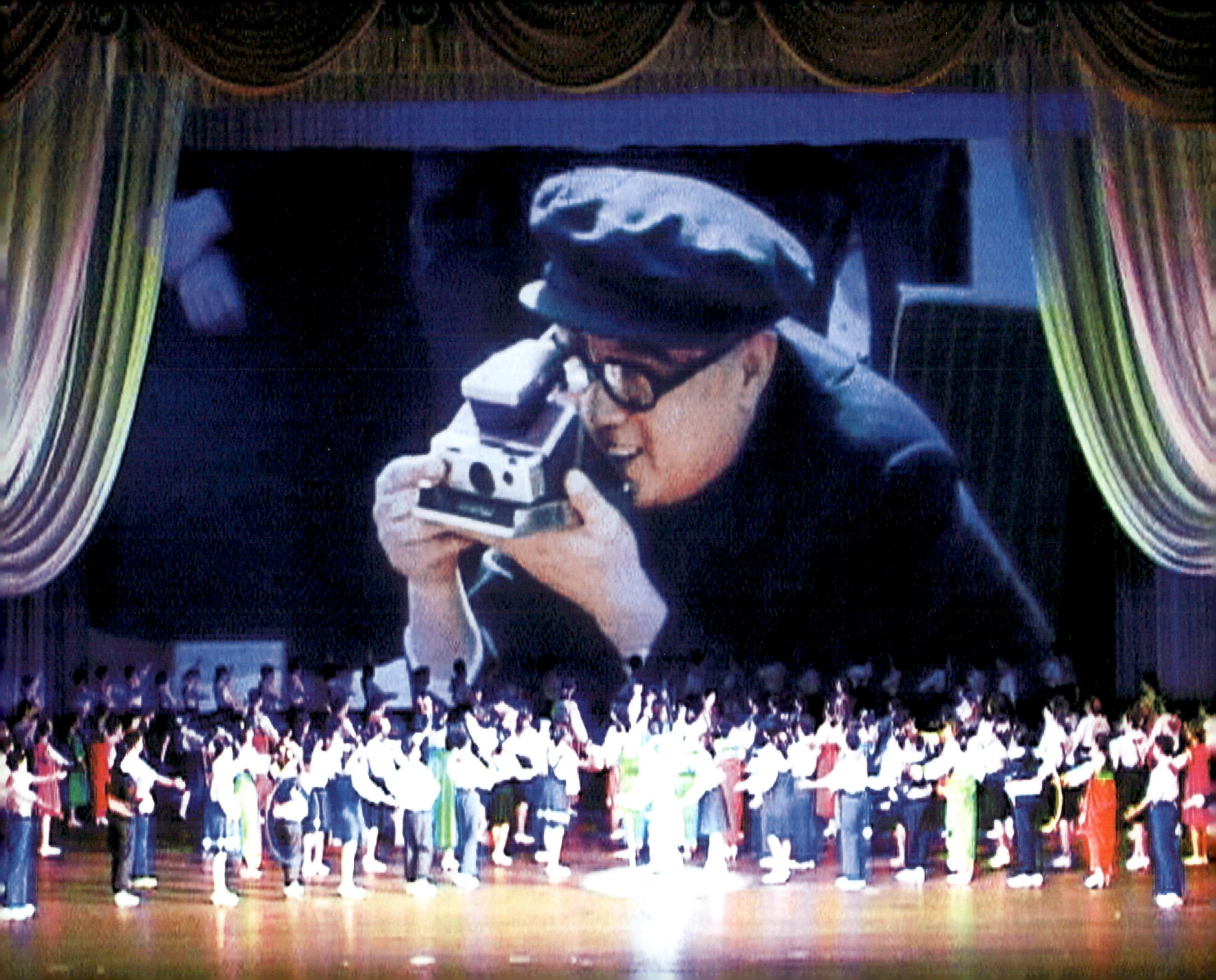

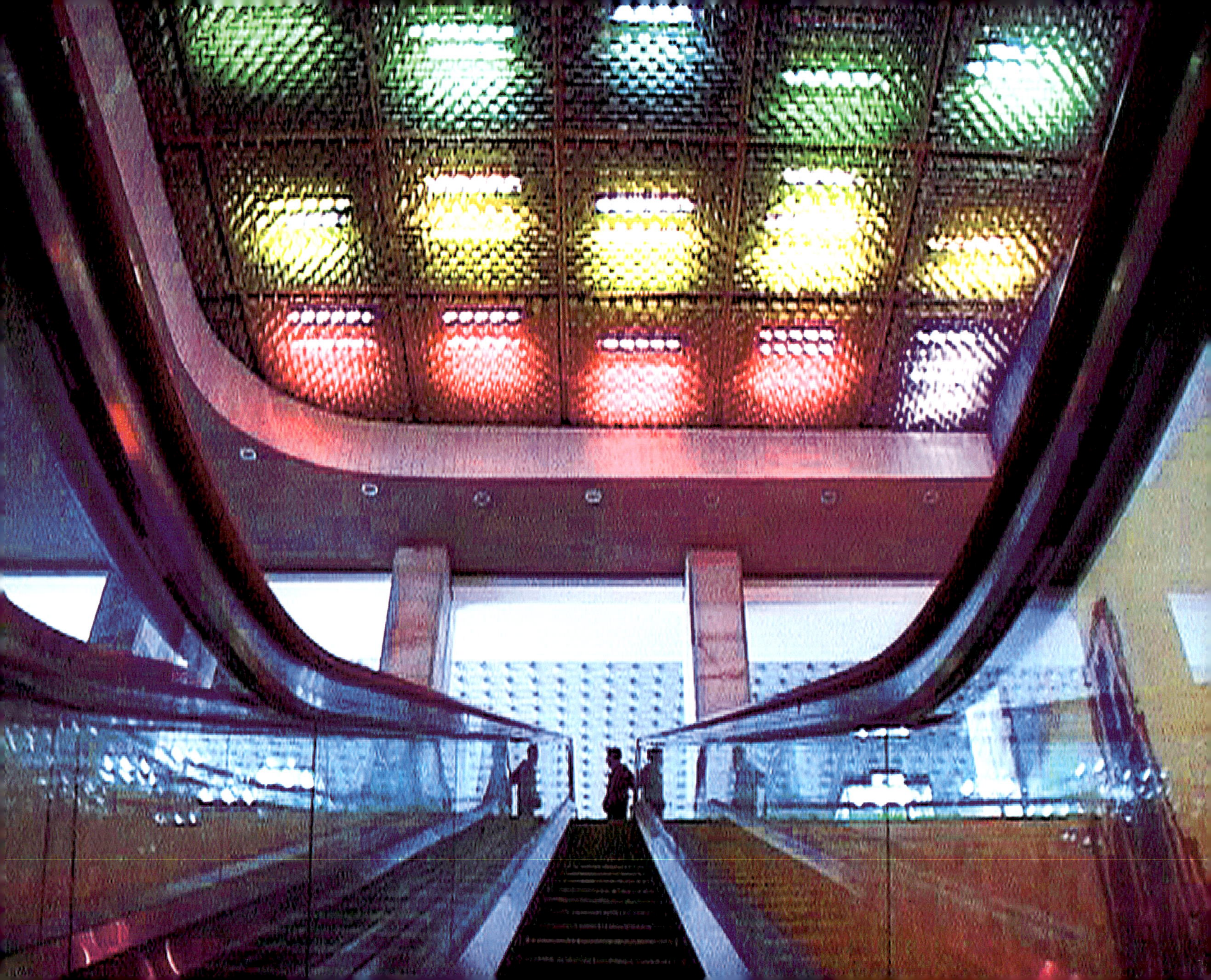

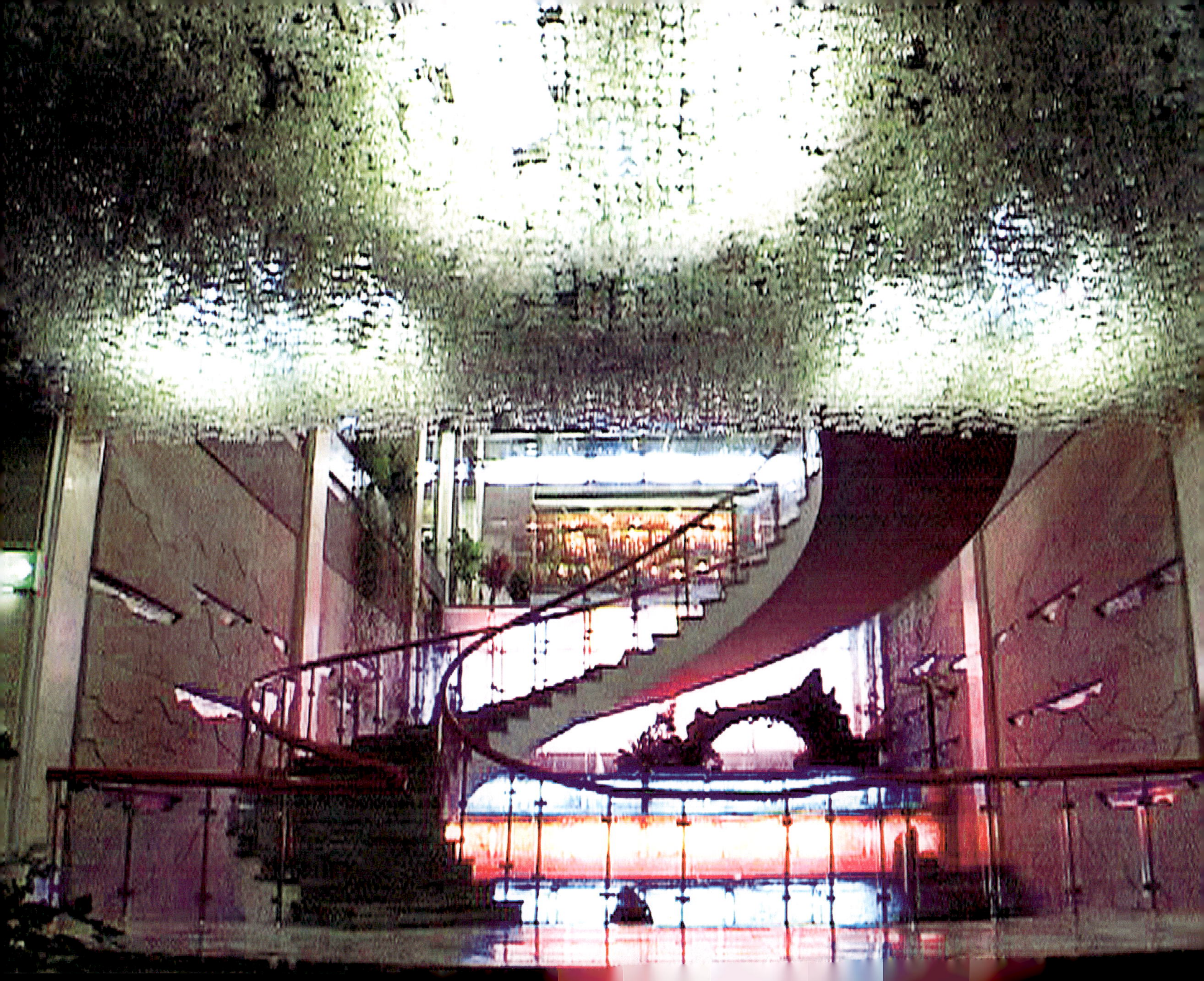

" Comrade Kim Il Sung is immortal. "

NEWS FROM PYONGYANG

YEAR 83 (JULY 8, 1994) **After ruling for forty-six years, Kim Il Sung dies from a heart attack. His son, Kim Jong Il succeeds him and becomes christened the "Dear Leader." As Kim Il Sung has been declared the "eternal president," Kim Jong Il takes on the title of "Chairman of the National Defense Commission."**

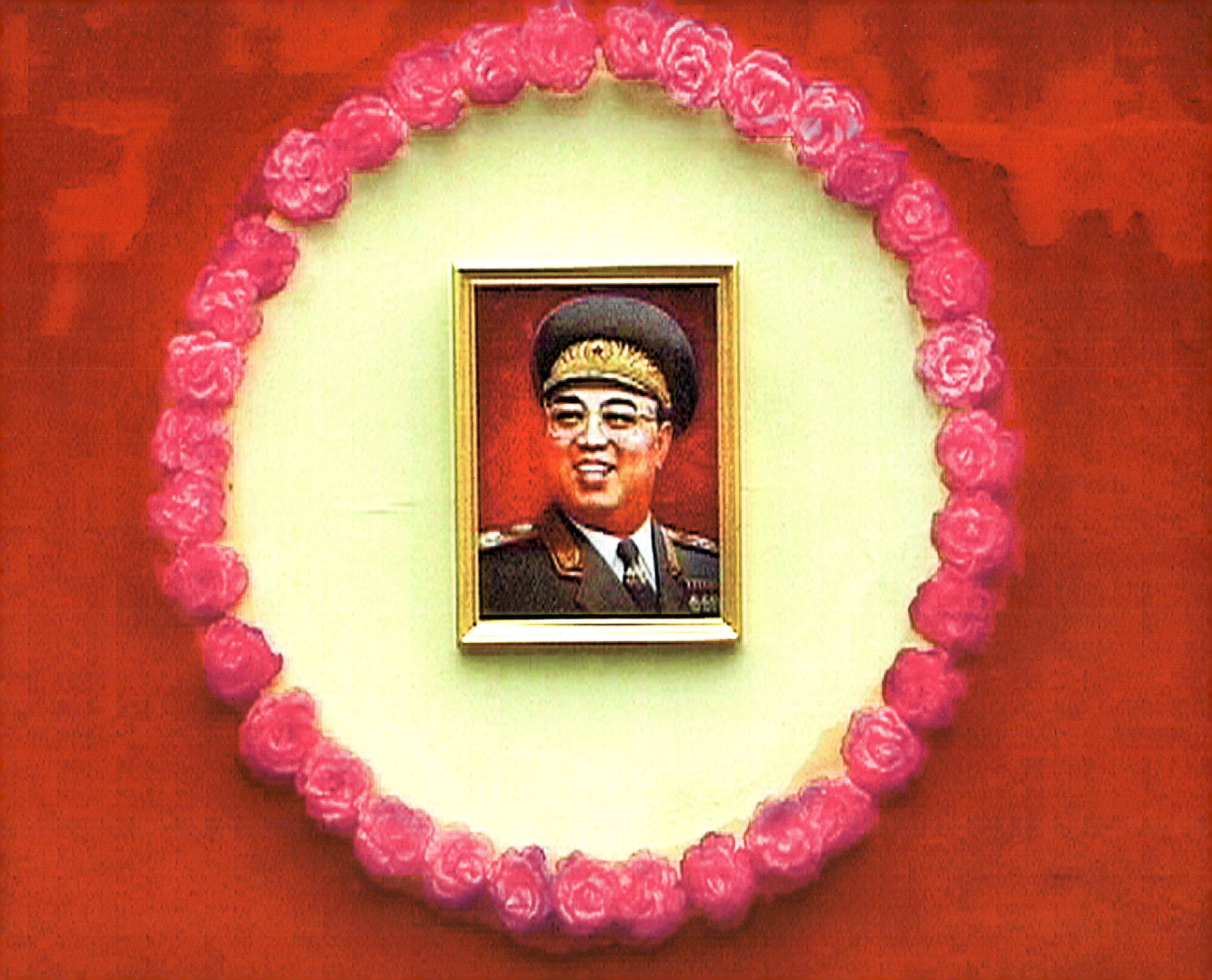

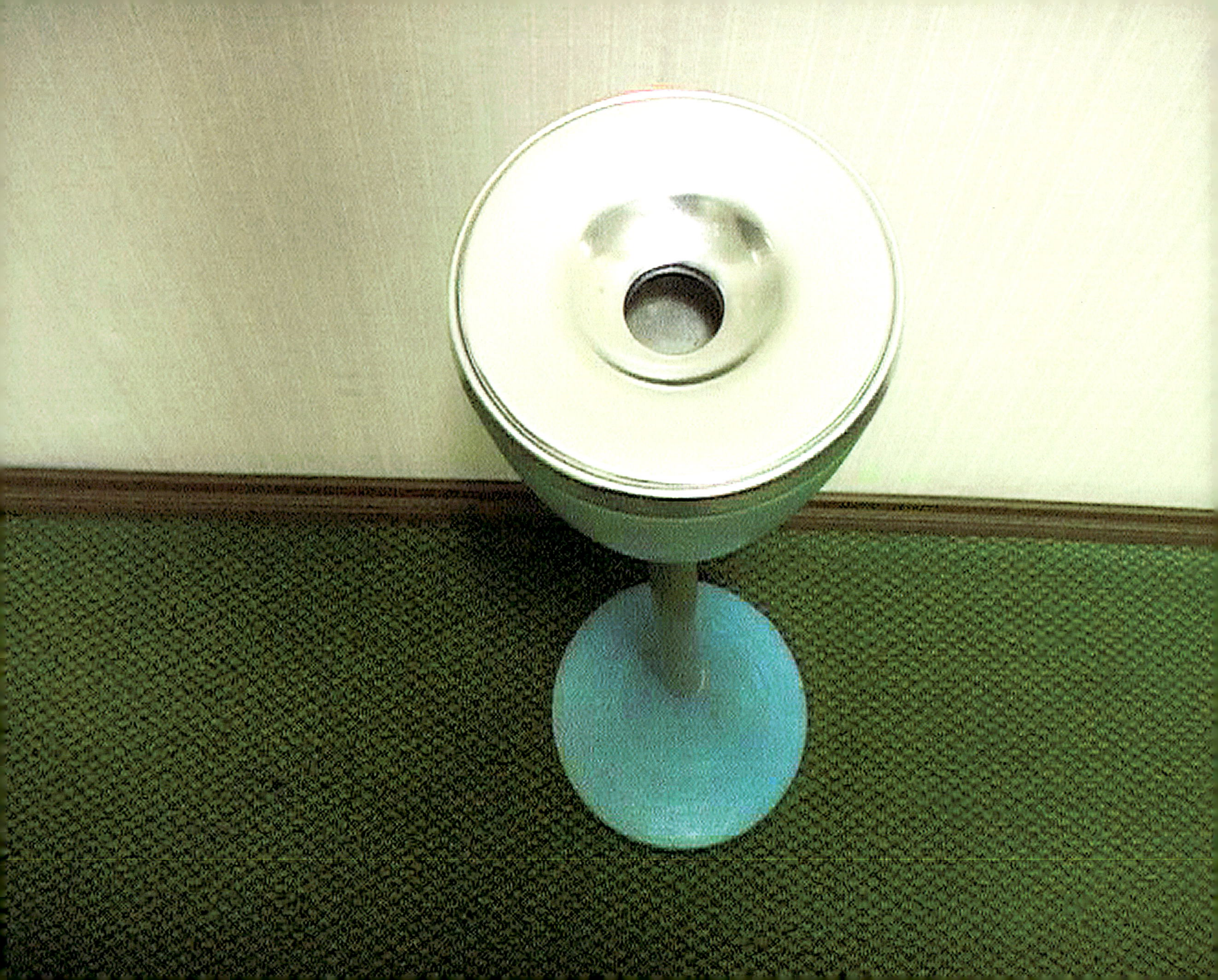

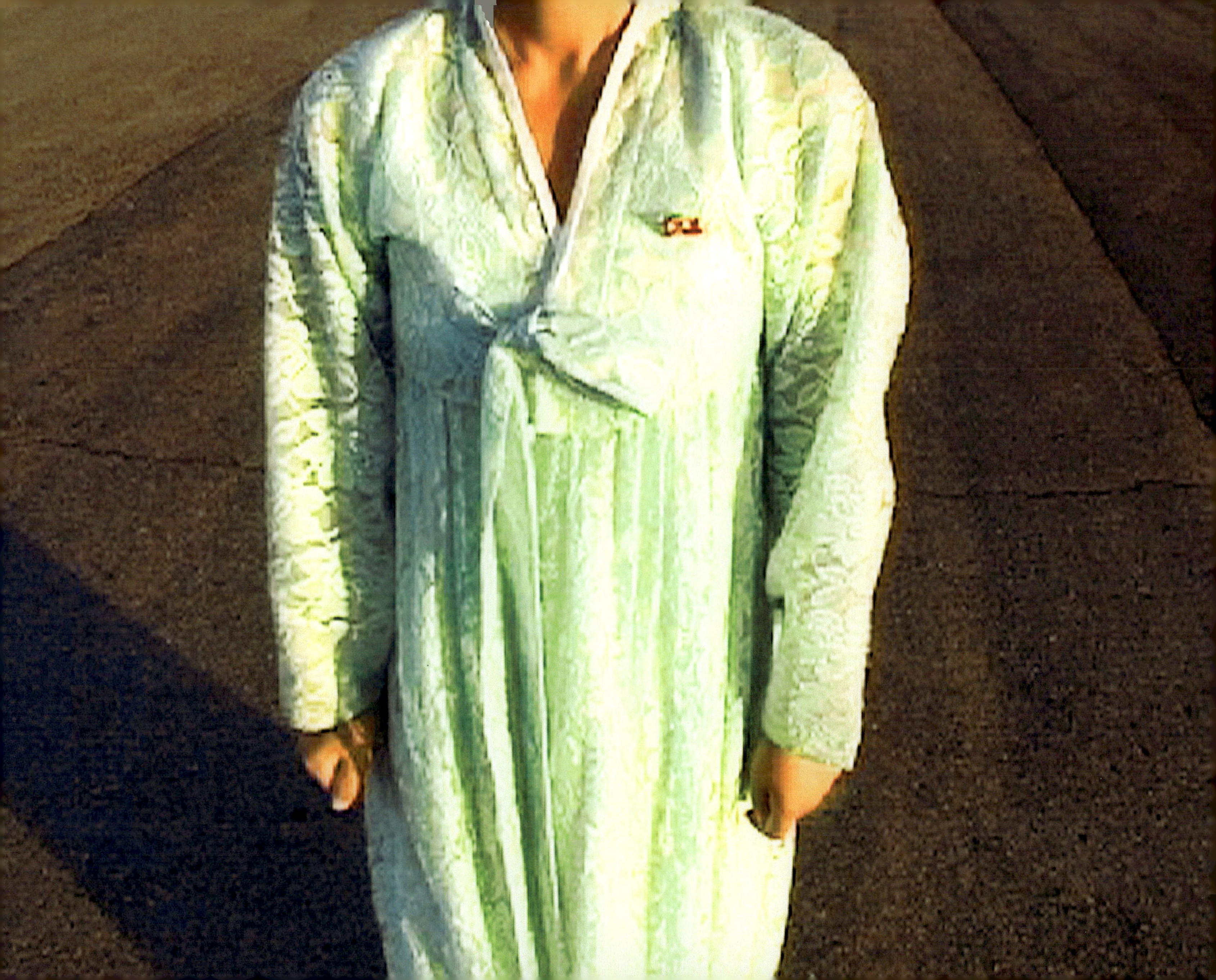

" Kim Jong Il is the perfect brain! "

SLOGAN IN THE STREETS OF PYONGYANG

YEAR 83 (OCTOBER 21, 1994) **North Korea and South Korea enter into the "Agreed Framework," which establishes that both countries will work toward a nuclear weapons-free Korean peninsula in exchange for heavy fuel oil for heating and electricity production.**

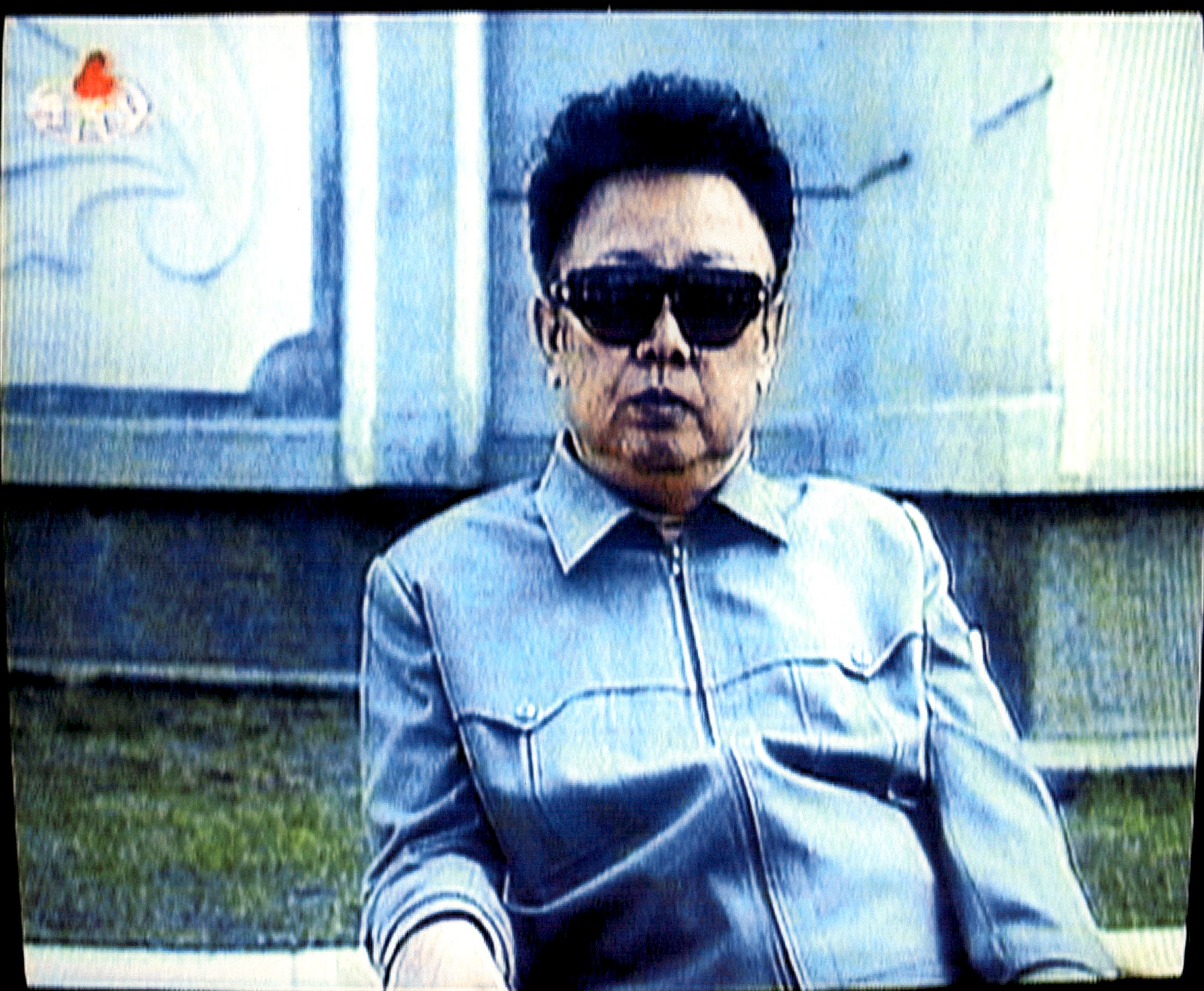

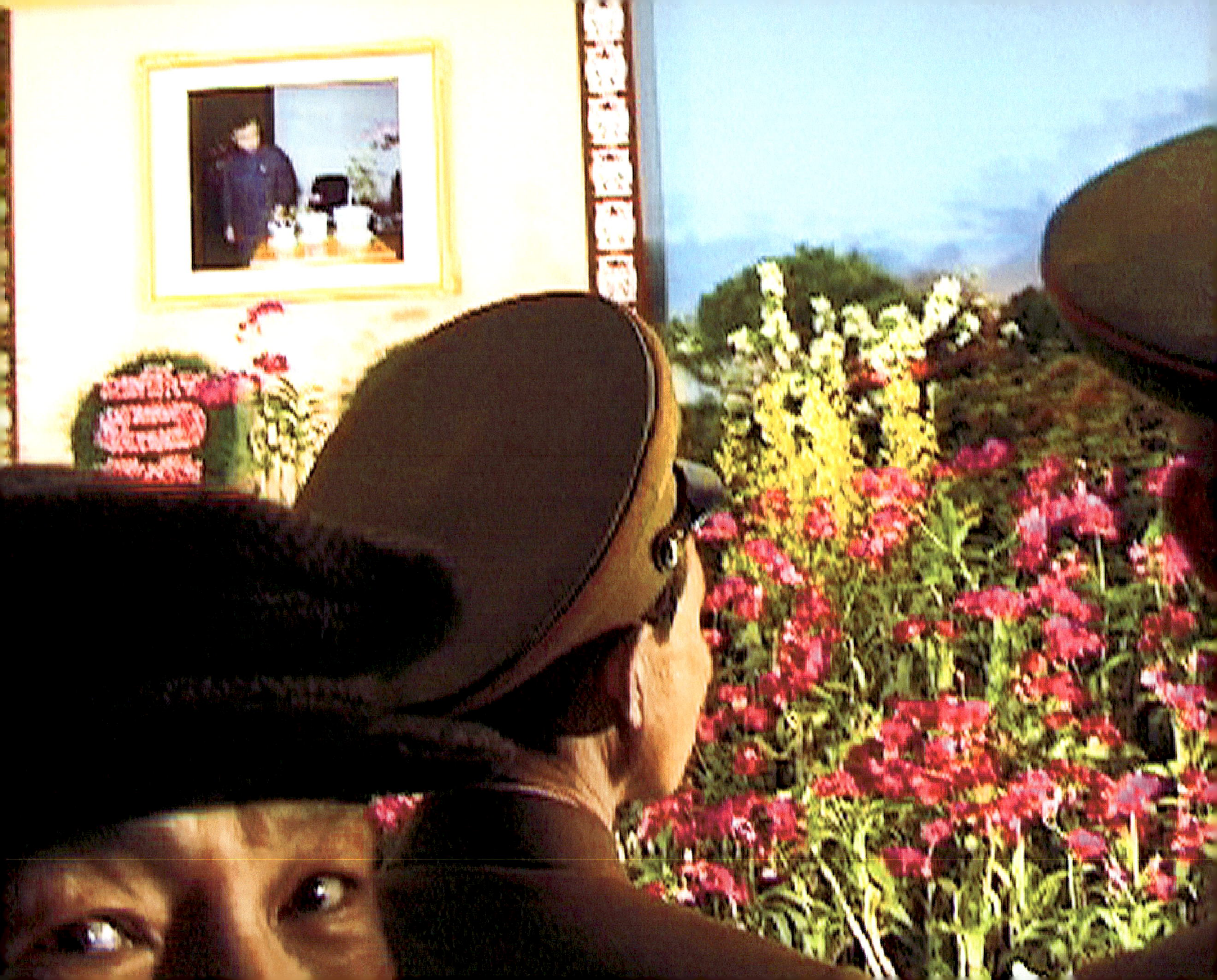

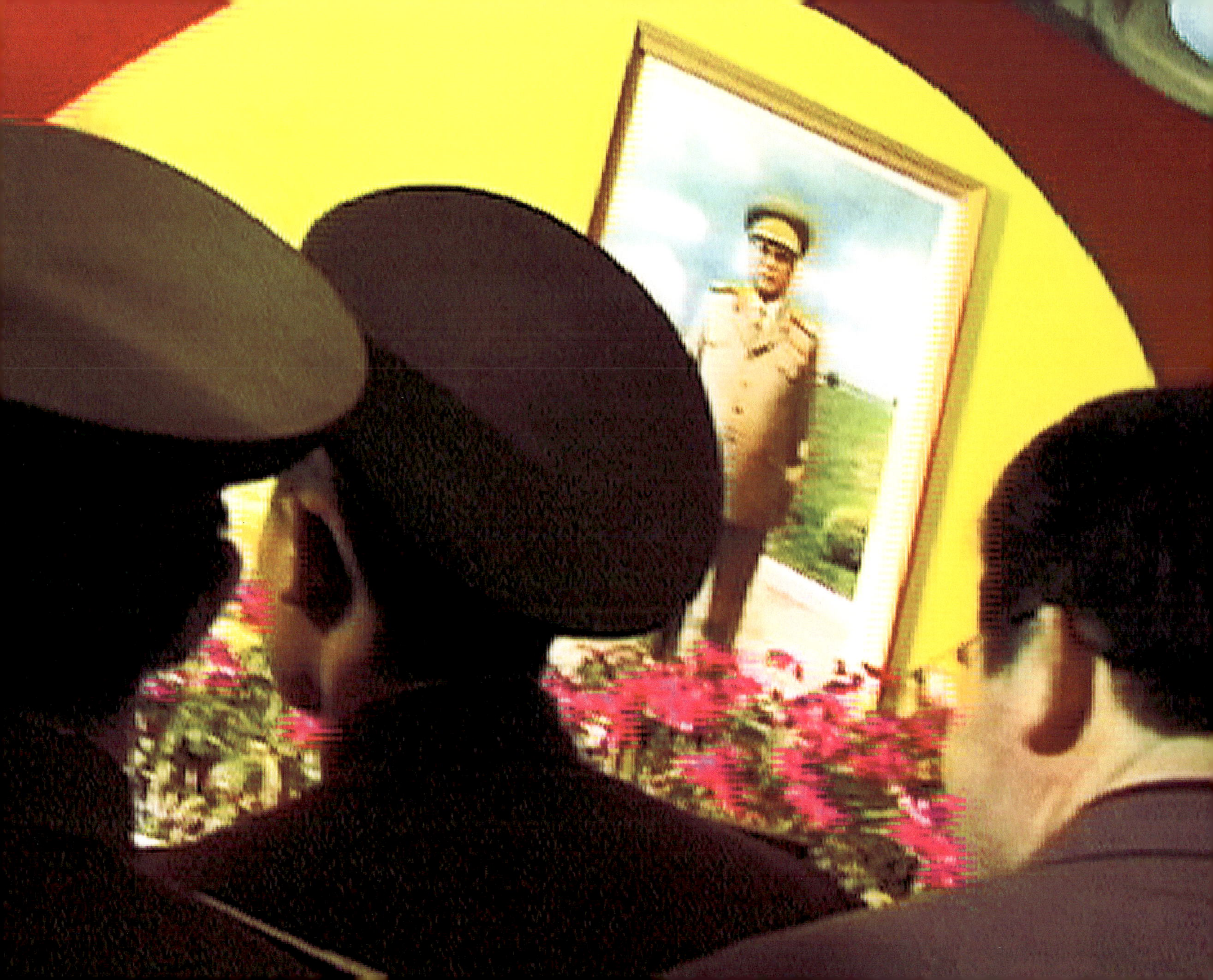

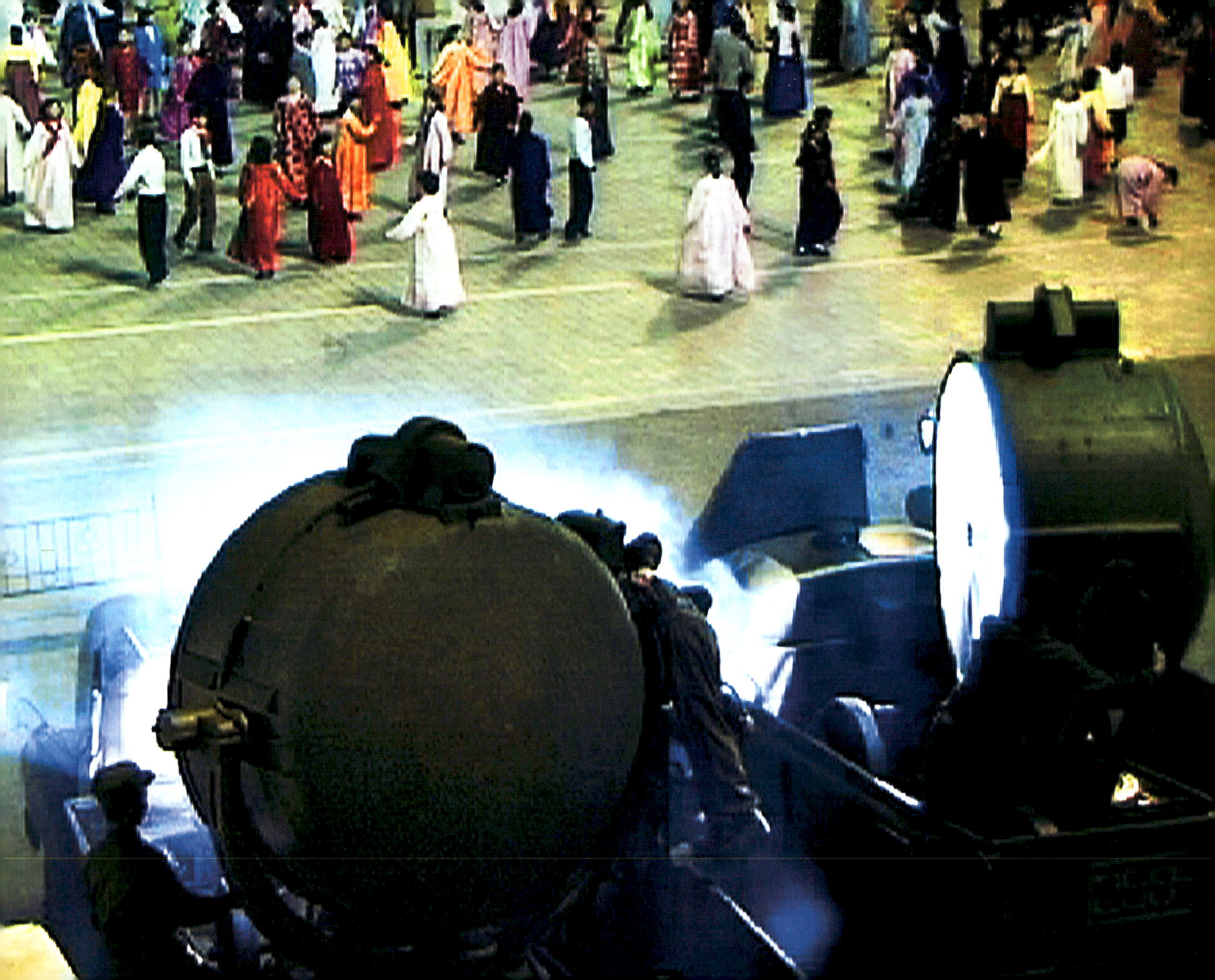

" The Sun Festival "

OFFICIAL GUIDE, HAN KIL HO

EVERY YEAR (APRIL 15) **North Koreans celebrate Kim Il Sung's birthday with an annual Sun Festival.**

" Rice is communism. "

KIM IL SUNG

YEAR 84 (JUNE 9, 1995) **North Korea falls prey to "natural disasters" and a deteriorating national economy, and makes its first appeal for international aid. The country is particularly in need of food.**

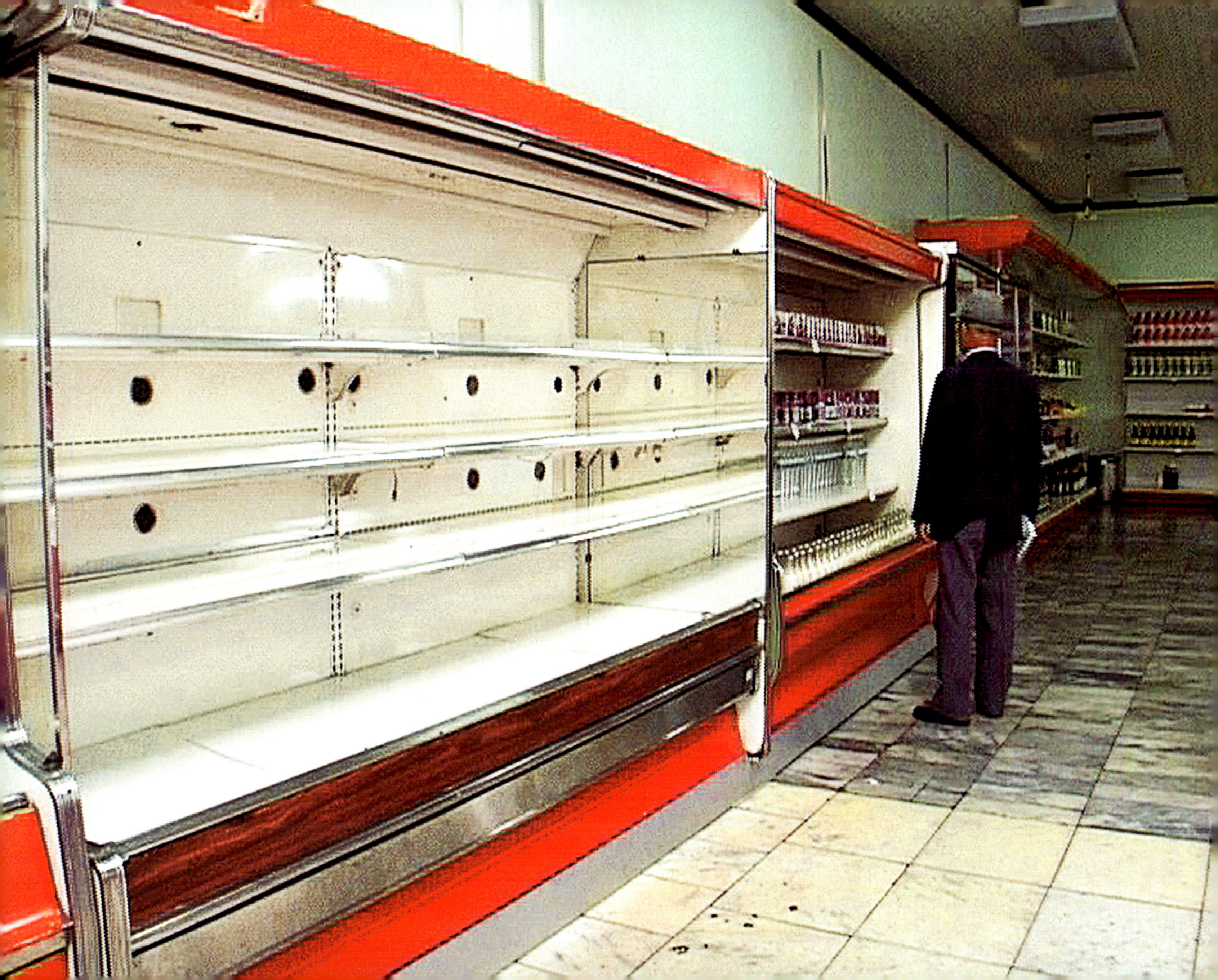

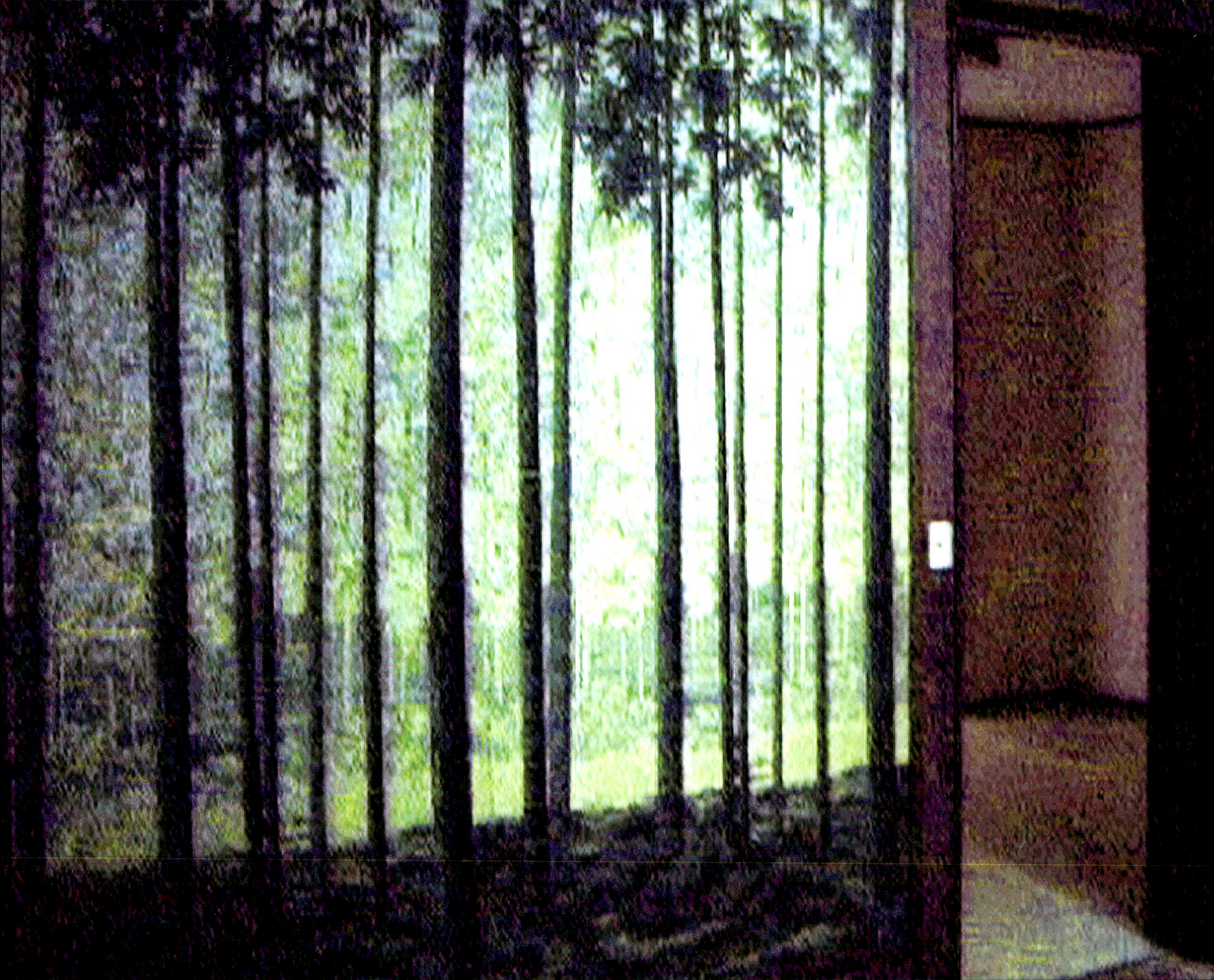

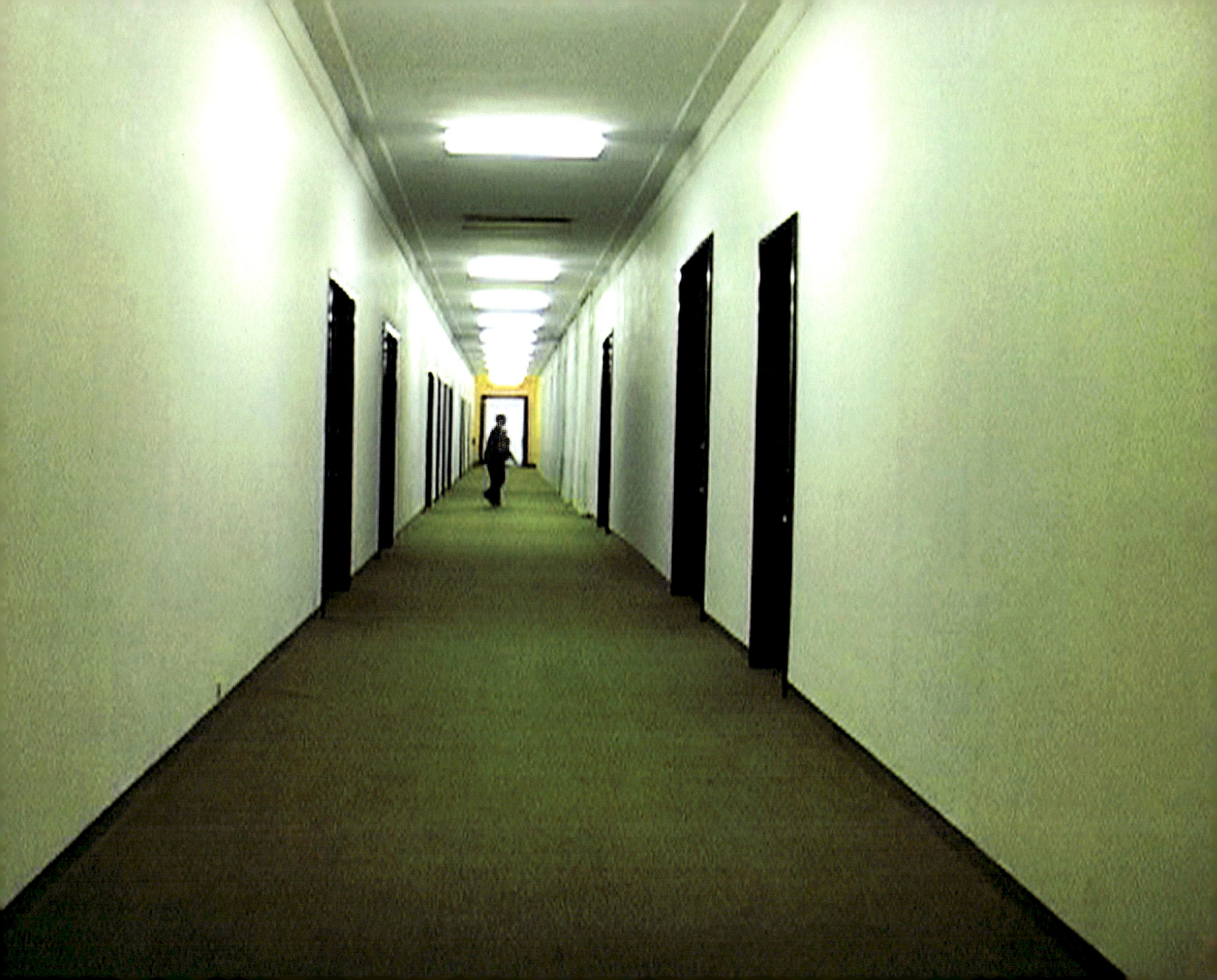

" Let us make miracles
on a worldwide scale,
with the same enthusiasm
as when we launch our satellite:
«Kwang-myangsong.» "

SLOGAN IN THE STREETS OF PYONGYANG

YEAR 87 (AUGUST 31, 1998) **North Korea test-fires a long-range ballistic missile over Japan. According to Pyongyang, the purpose of this operation is to put a satellite into orbit to broadcast North Korean revolutionary songs from outer space to glorify Kim Il Sung.**

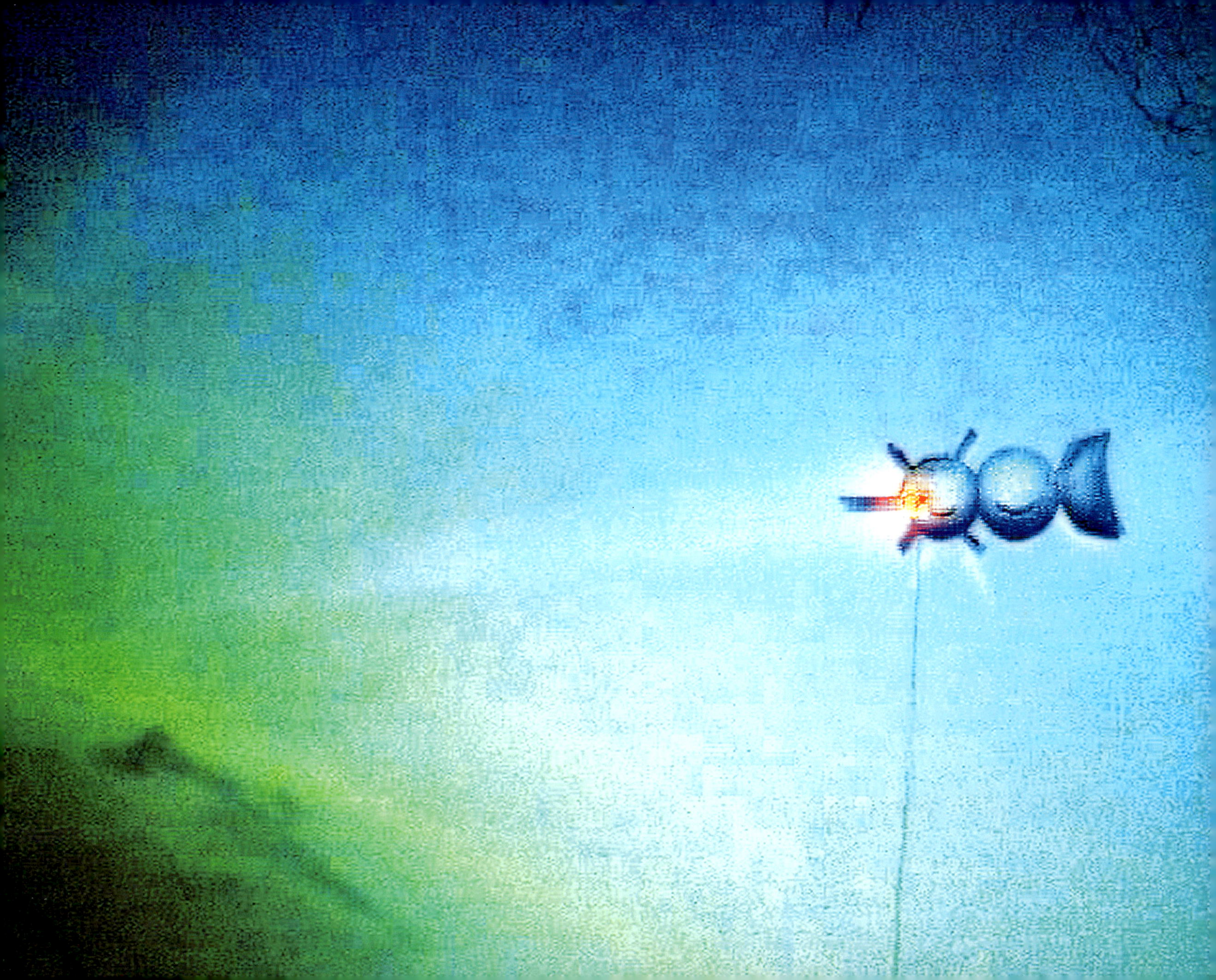

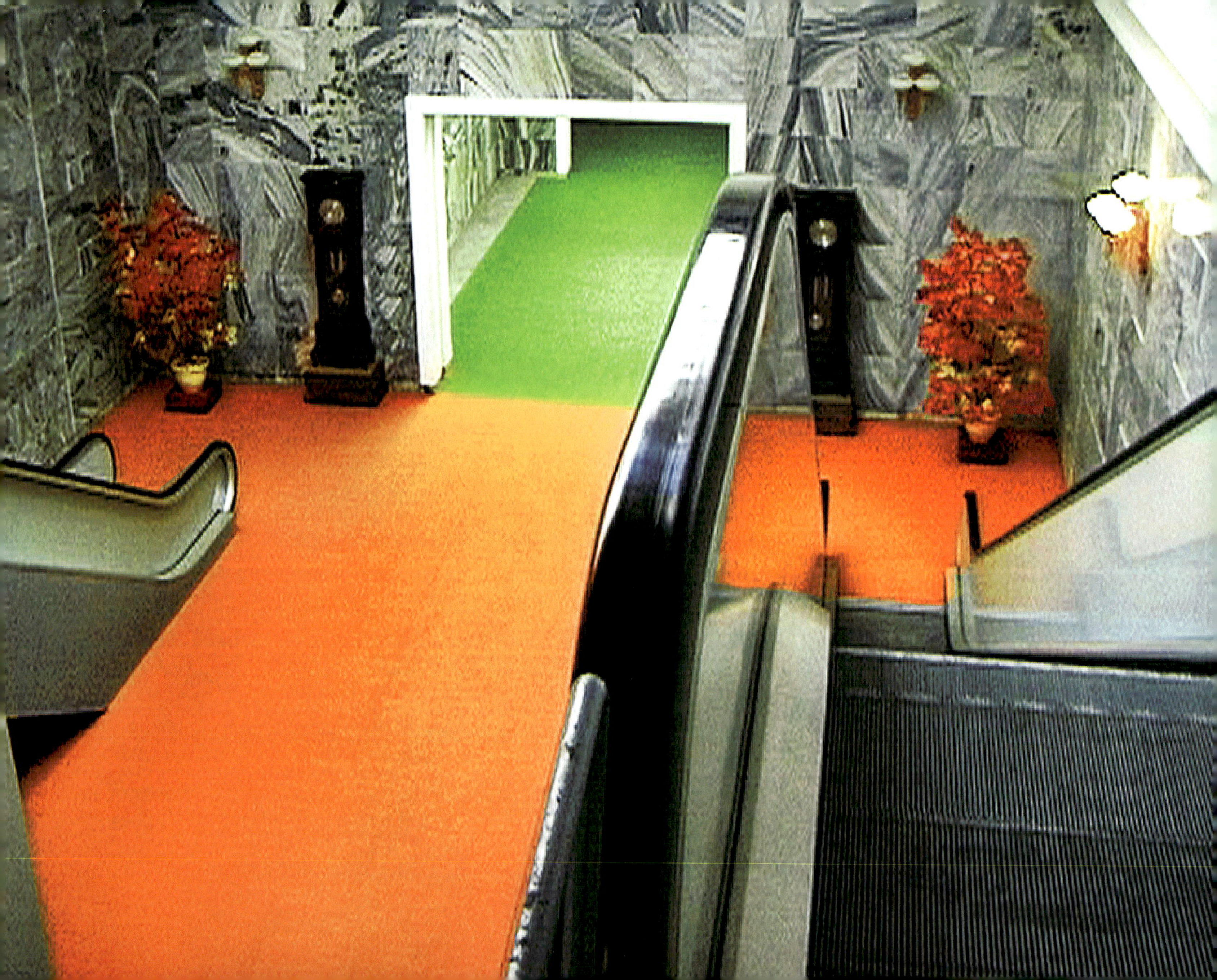

" Korea is one. "

PYONGYANG FOREIGN LANGUAGE EDITION

YEAR 89 (JUNE 14, 2000) **First historic summit takes place between the Leaders of North and South Korea. The presidents sign the joint North-South declaration in Pyongyang. The latter calls upon both countries to combine efforts to facilitate national reunification.**

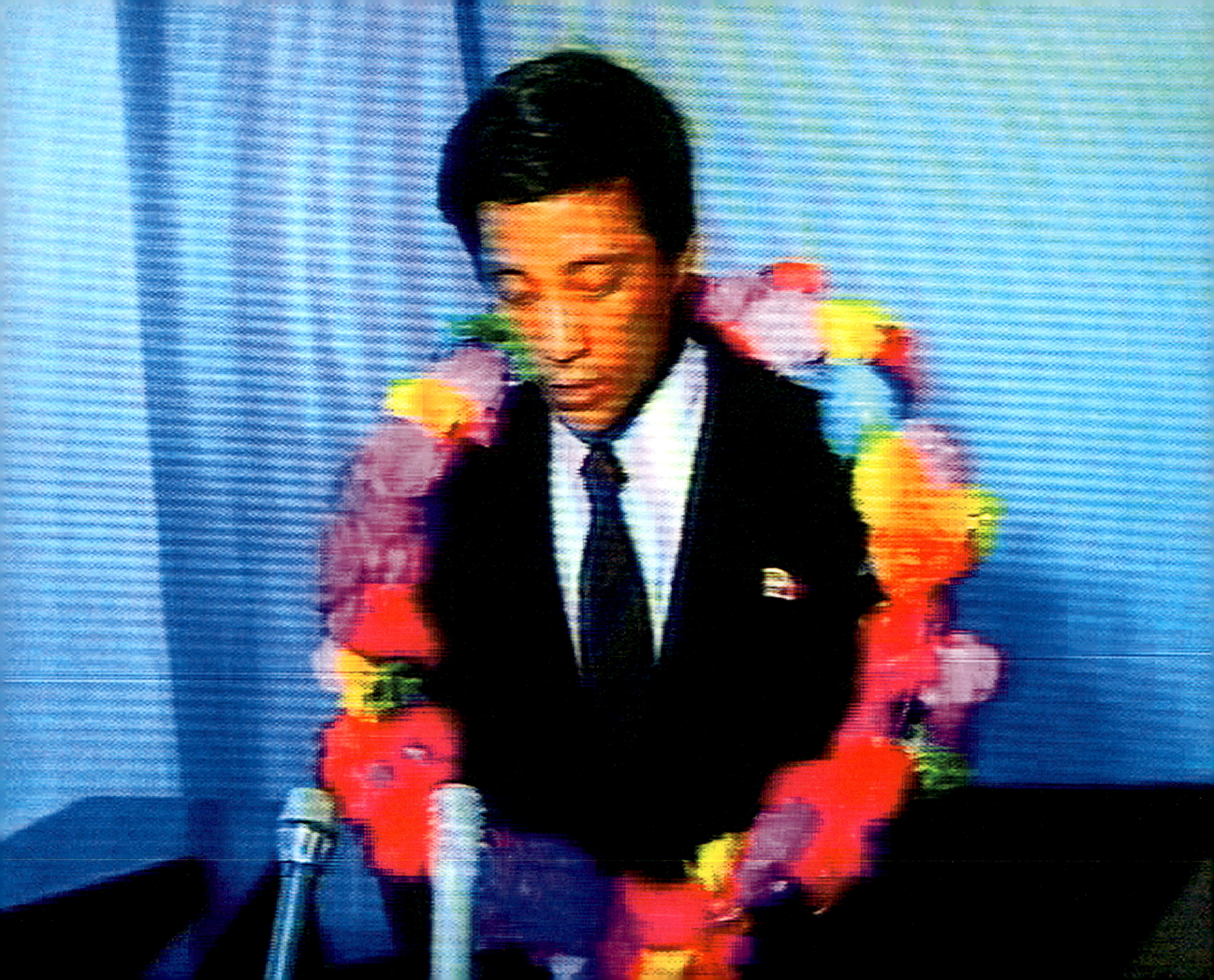

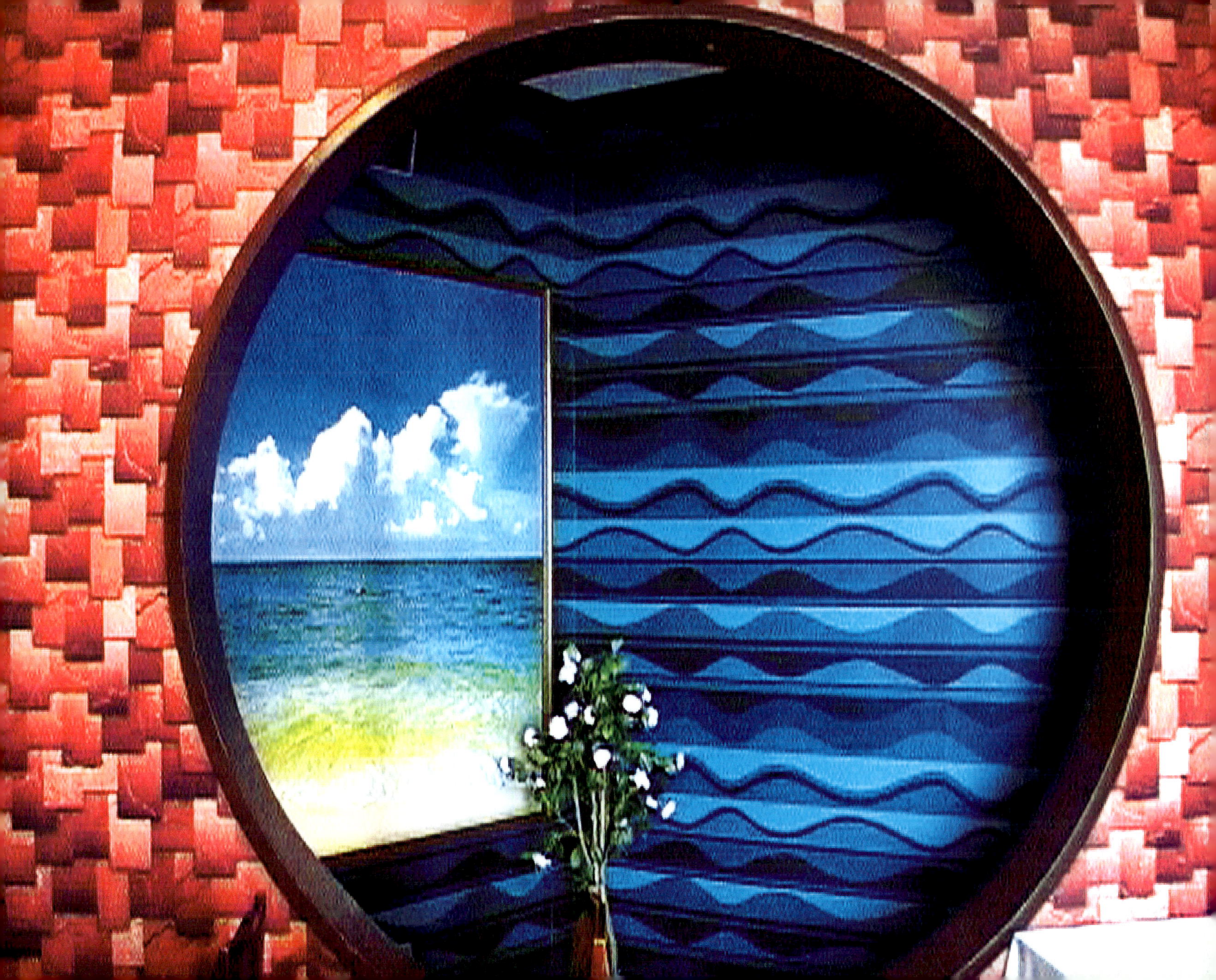

" A statue made of gold for those who find oil. "

KIM IL SUNG

~~YEAR 89 (DECEMBER 12, 2000) **The International Federation of the Red Cross warns that North Korea faces a health crisis as well as famine.**~~

YEAR 89 (MAY 15, 2001) **A North Korean member of Office No. 39 of the Department of the Economy starts a rumour that an oil well at Saetbyol Gun has a potential of one billion tons.**

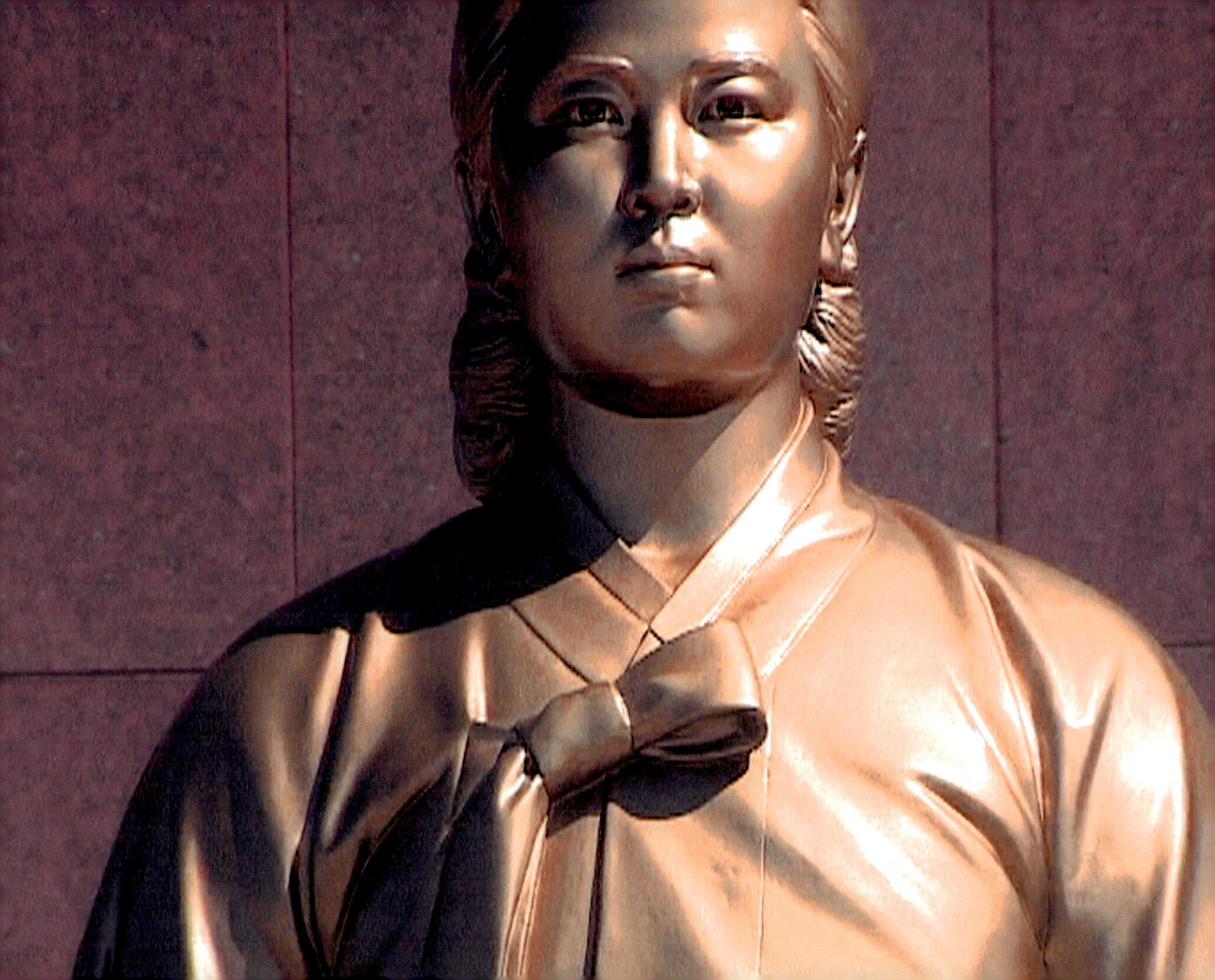

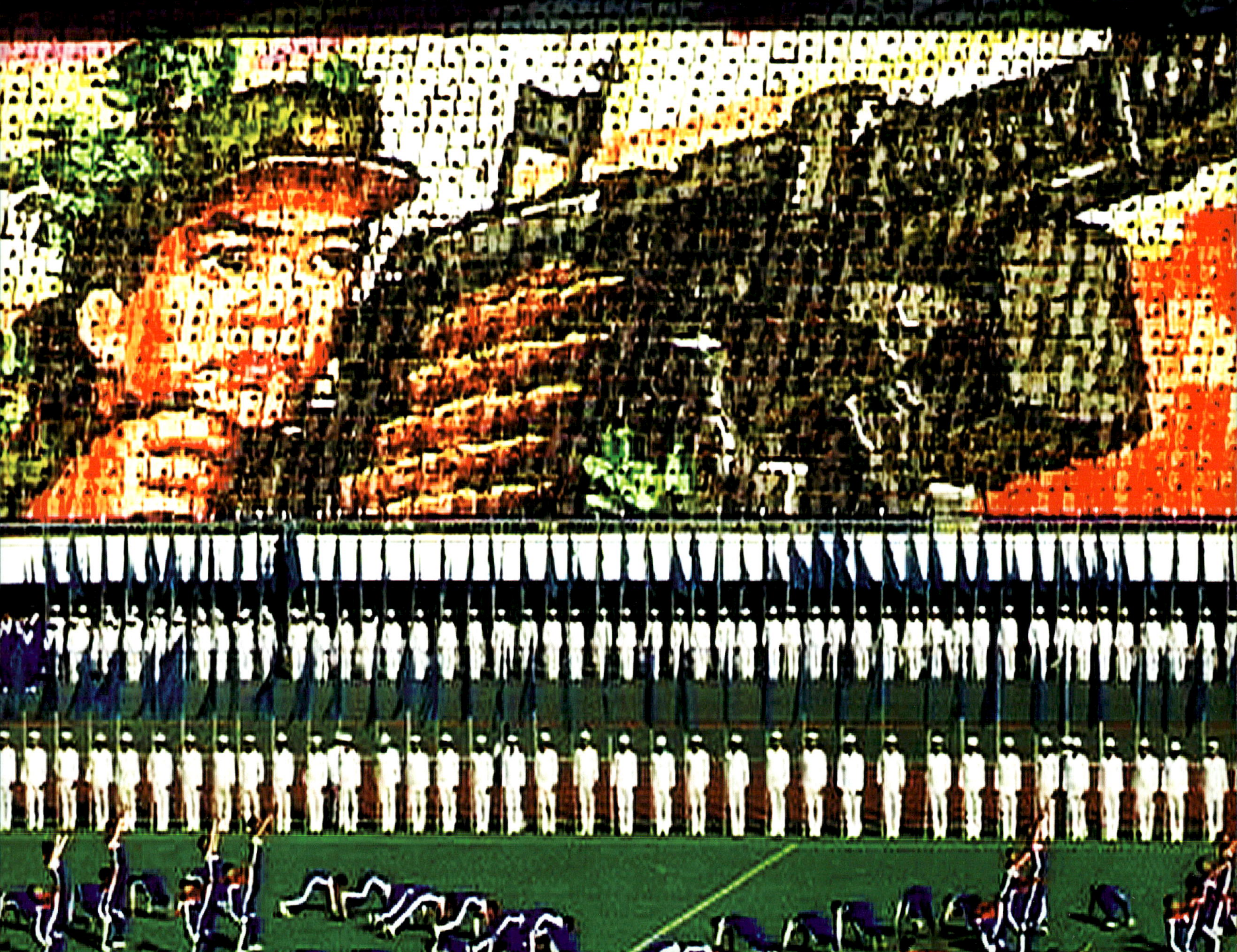

" This is almost a declaration of war. "

SPOKESMAN FOR THE MINISTRY OF FOREIGN AFFAIRS IN NORTH KOREA

YEAR 91 (JANUARY 29, 2002) **The United States declares that North Korea is part of an "Axis of Evil." It reproaches North Korea with "arming itself with missiles and weapons of mass destruction which, with the help of their terrorist allies, is a threat to world peace."**

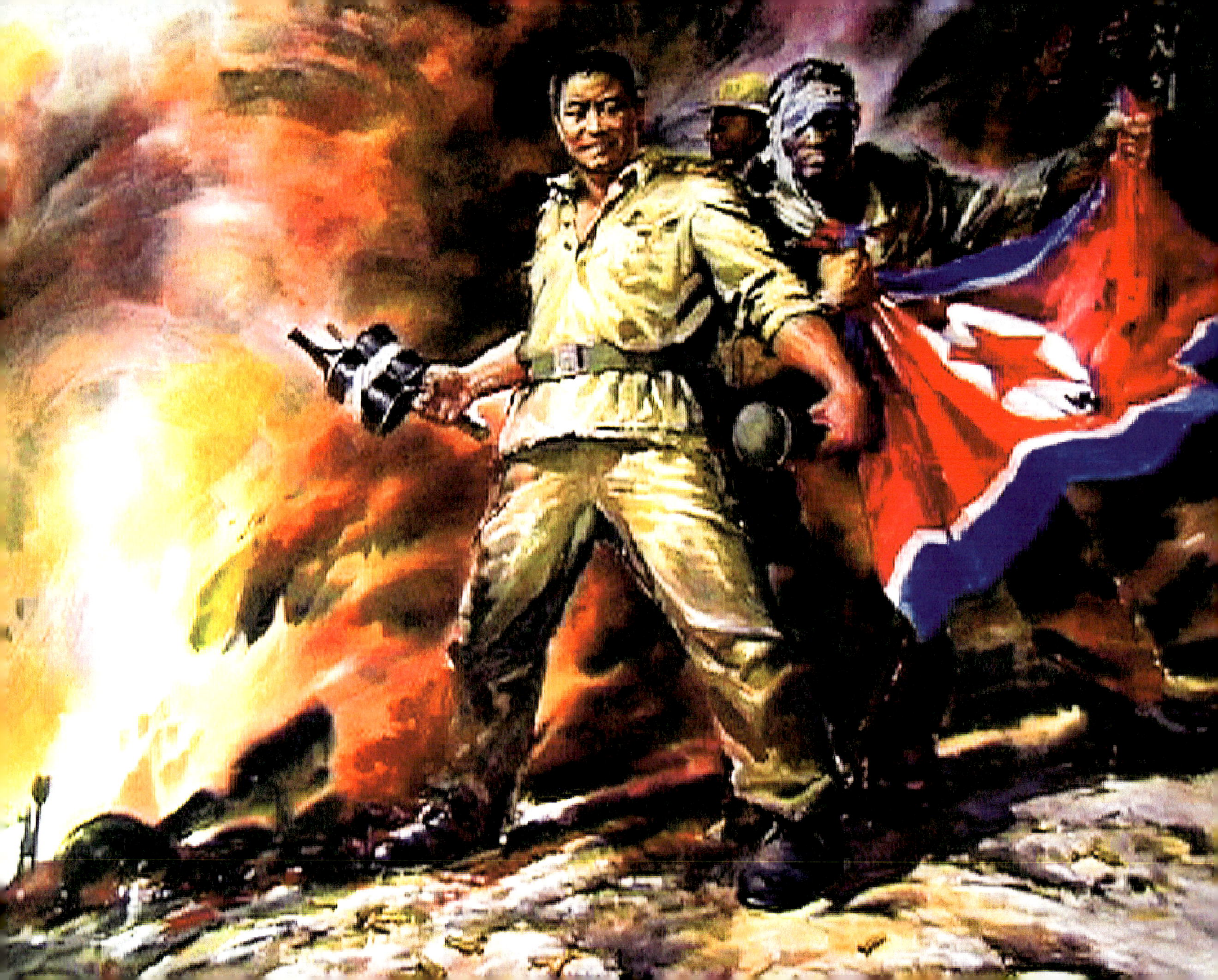

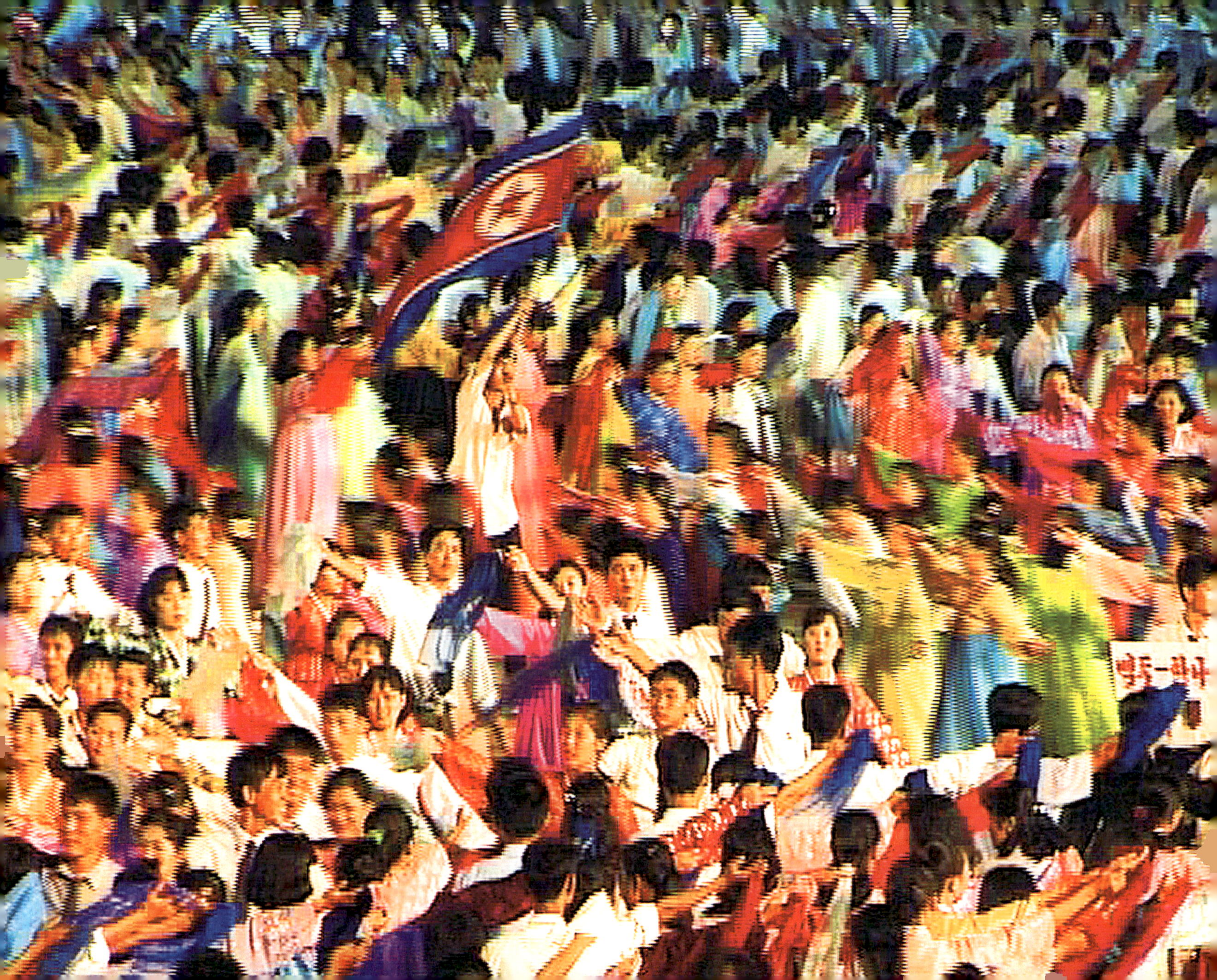

" Naval war in the yellow sea "

NEWS FROM PYONGYANG

YEAR 91 (JUNE 29, 2002) **Two North Korean gunboats escorting fishing boats cross into South Korean territorial waters. Using a loud speaker the South Korean navy asks them to turn back. In response, the North Koreans open fire, leaving four dead, nineteen injured and one missing among the South Koreans, and about thirty North Koreans wounded. Both countries mutually accuse the other of opening fire.**

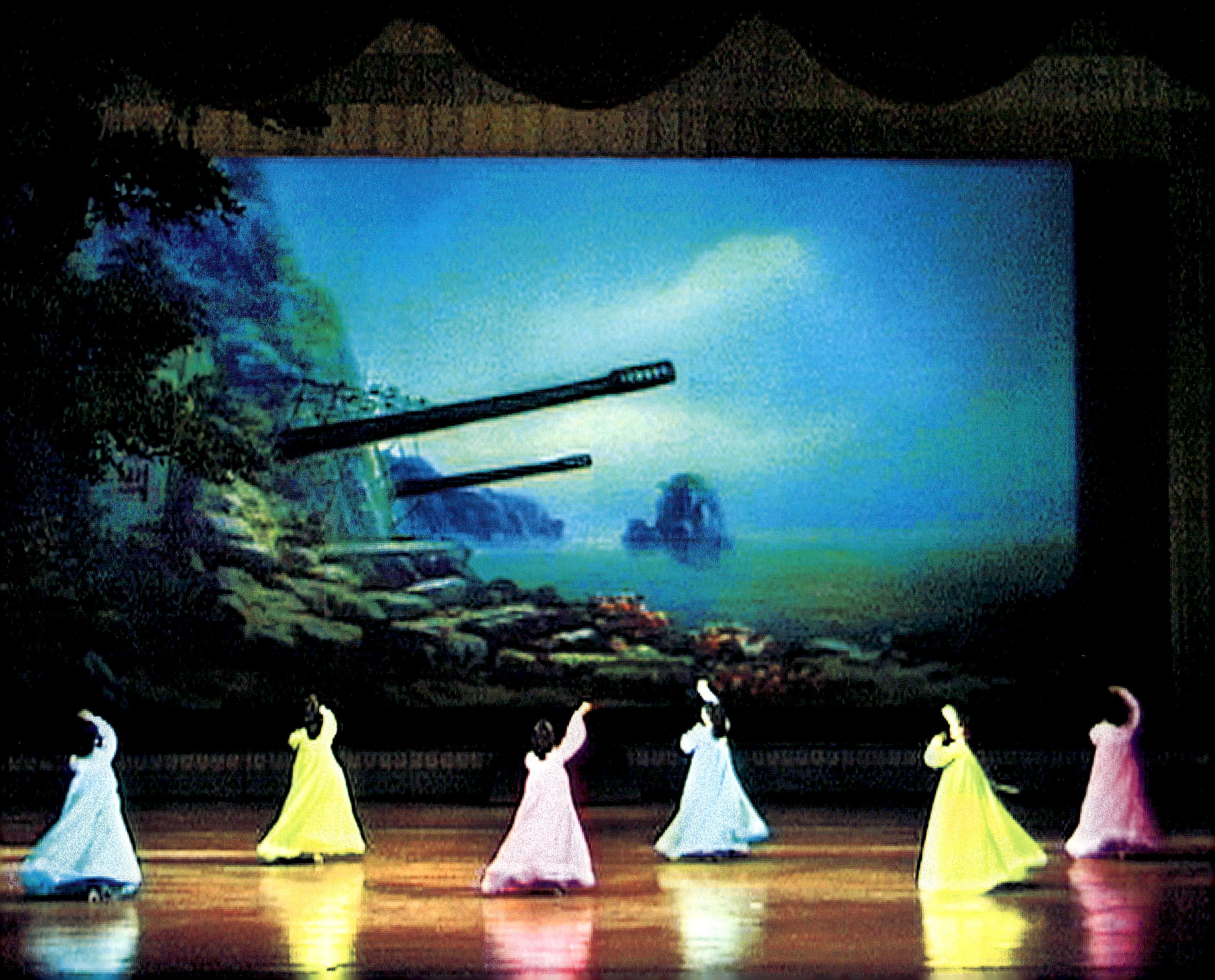

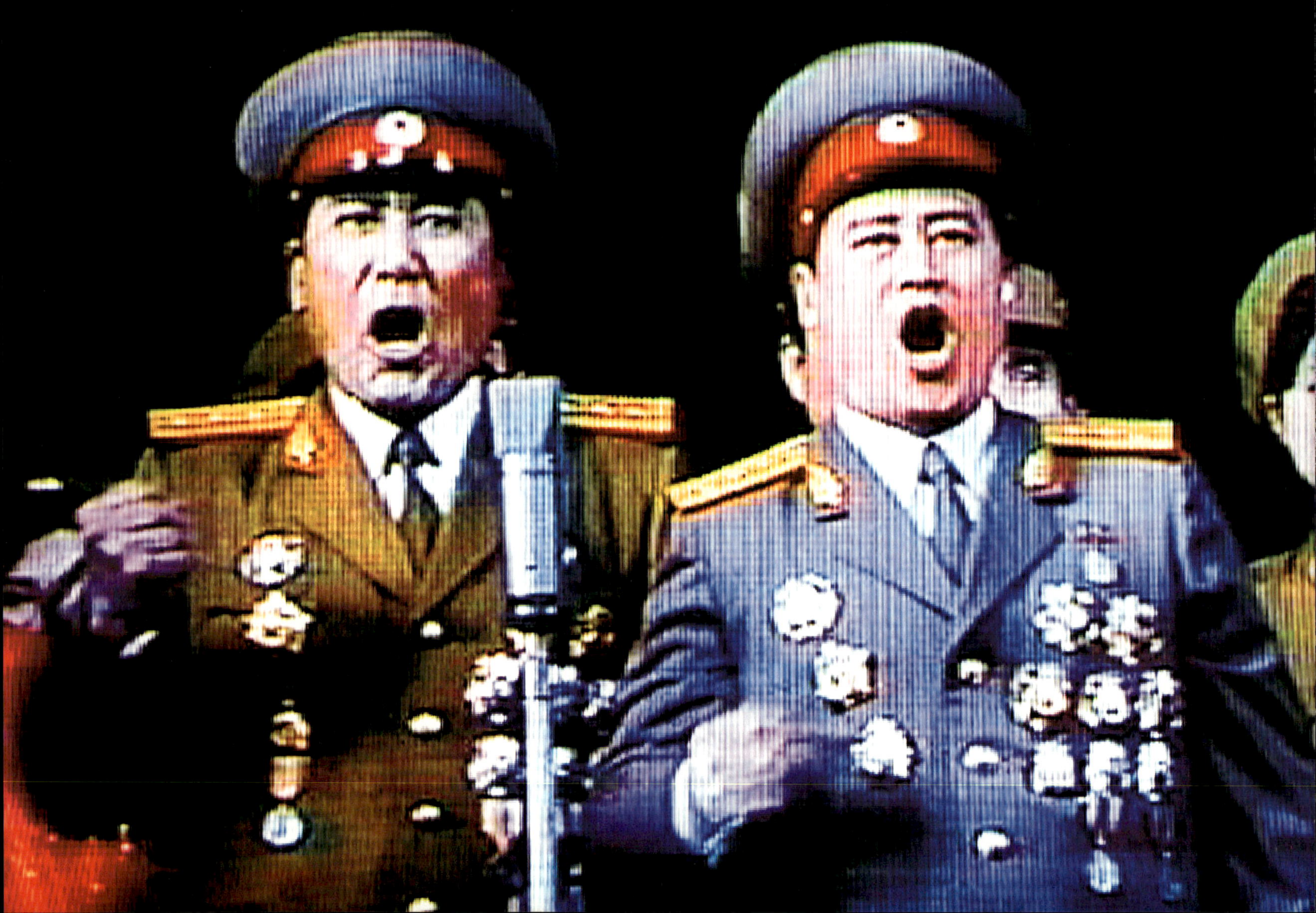

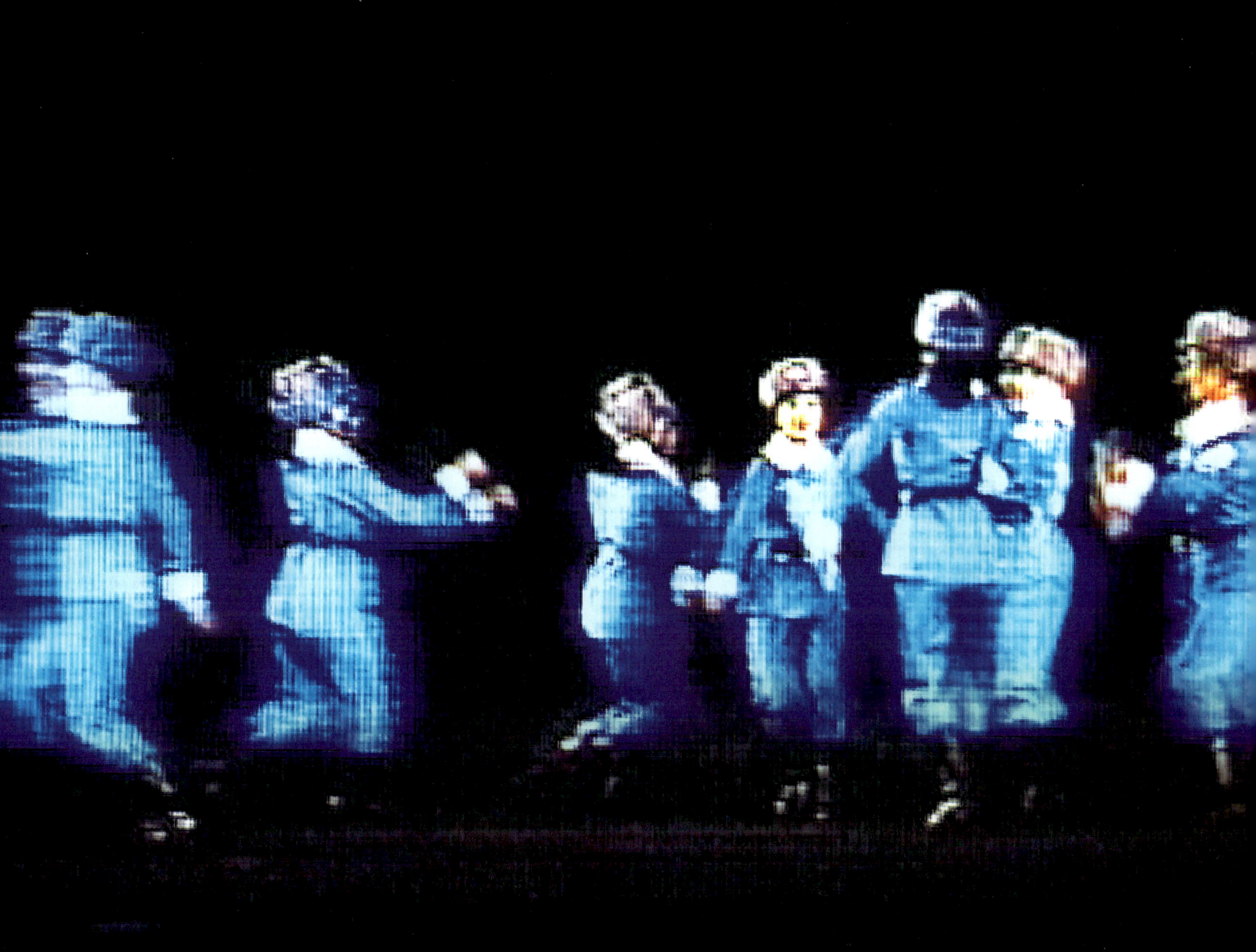

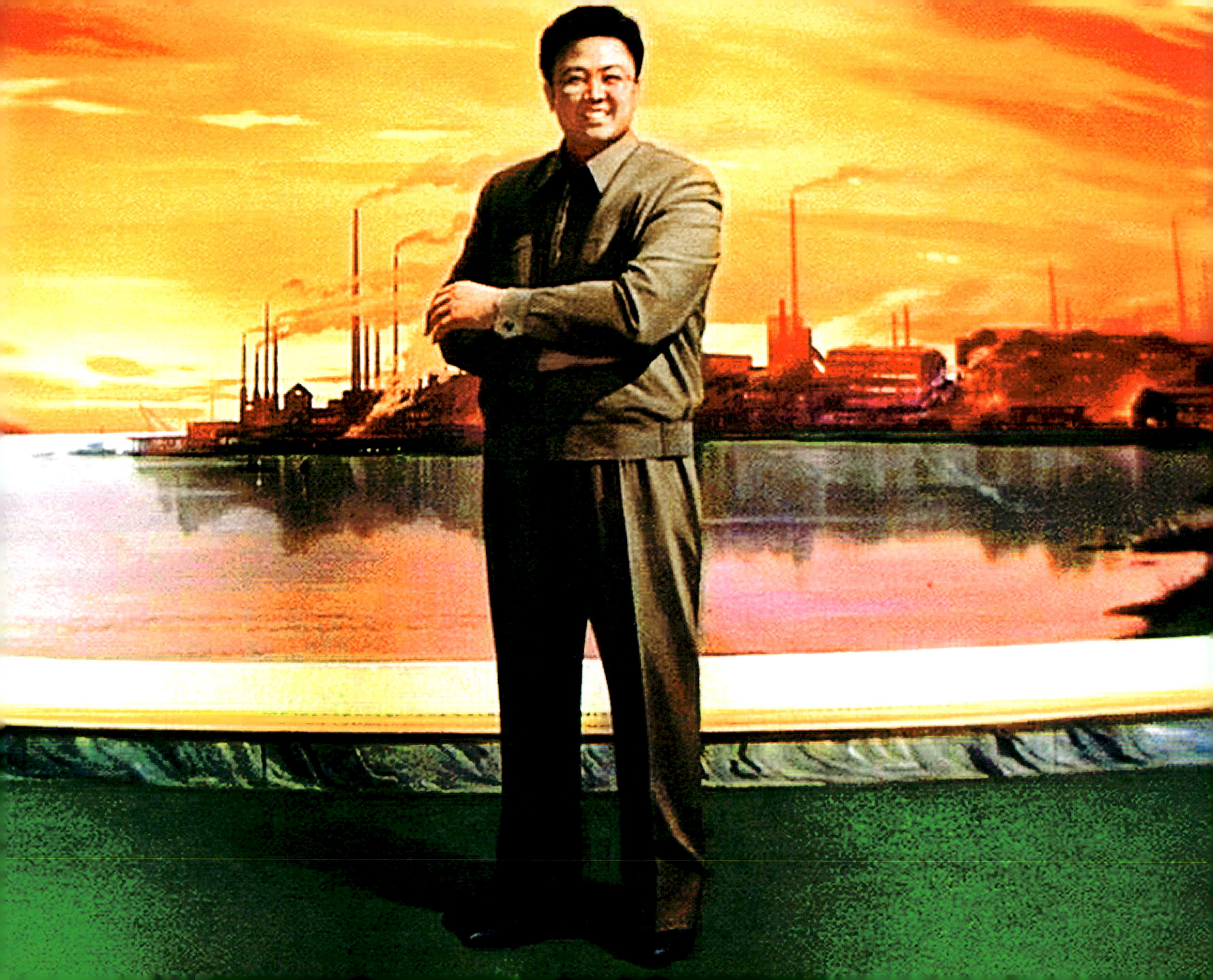

" We kidnapped some Japanese. "

KIM JONG IL

YEAR 91 (SEPTEMBER 17, 2002) **During a visit to Pyongyang by Japanese Prime Minister Junichiro Koizumi, Kim Jong Il apologizes for the systematic kidnapping of Japanese citizens which took place between 1977 and 1983, undertaken to train its spies "after the Japanese way of life" in order to infiltrate the Japanese archipelago.**

" We are ready to launch a nuclear attack against the United States. "

KIM JONG IL

YEAR 91 (OCTOBER 22, 2002) **North Korea admits to having nuclear weapons, which violates the agreement of 1994. Kim Jong Il declares that he "is ready to launch a nuclear attack against the United States by involving Japan and South Korea" and that "U.S. nuclear supremacy could only be proved through an atomic war." In terms of declared nuclear powers worldwide, North Korea ranks ninth. Its arsenal of ground missiles includes modified Scuds which could threaten South Korea and Japan. The Taepodong 3 missile, currently being developed, has a range approaching 6,000 km, which means North Korea could threaten Alaska and Hawaïi.**

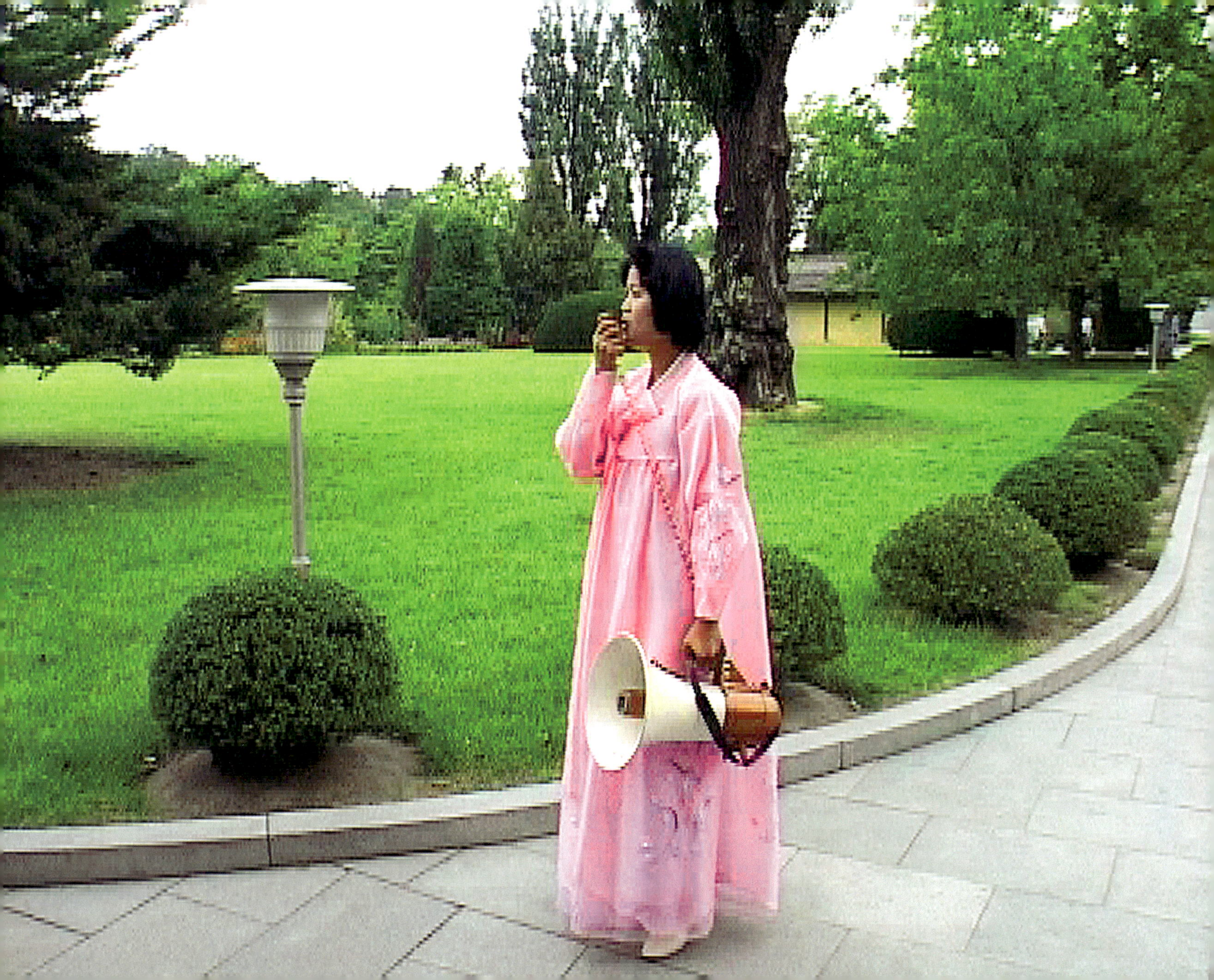

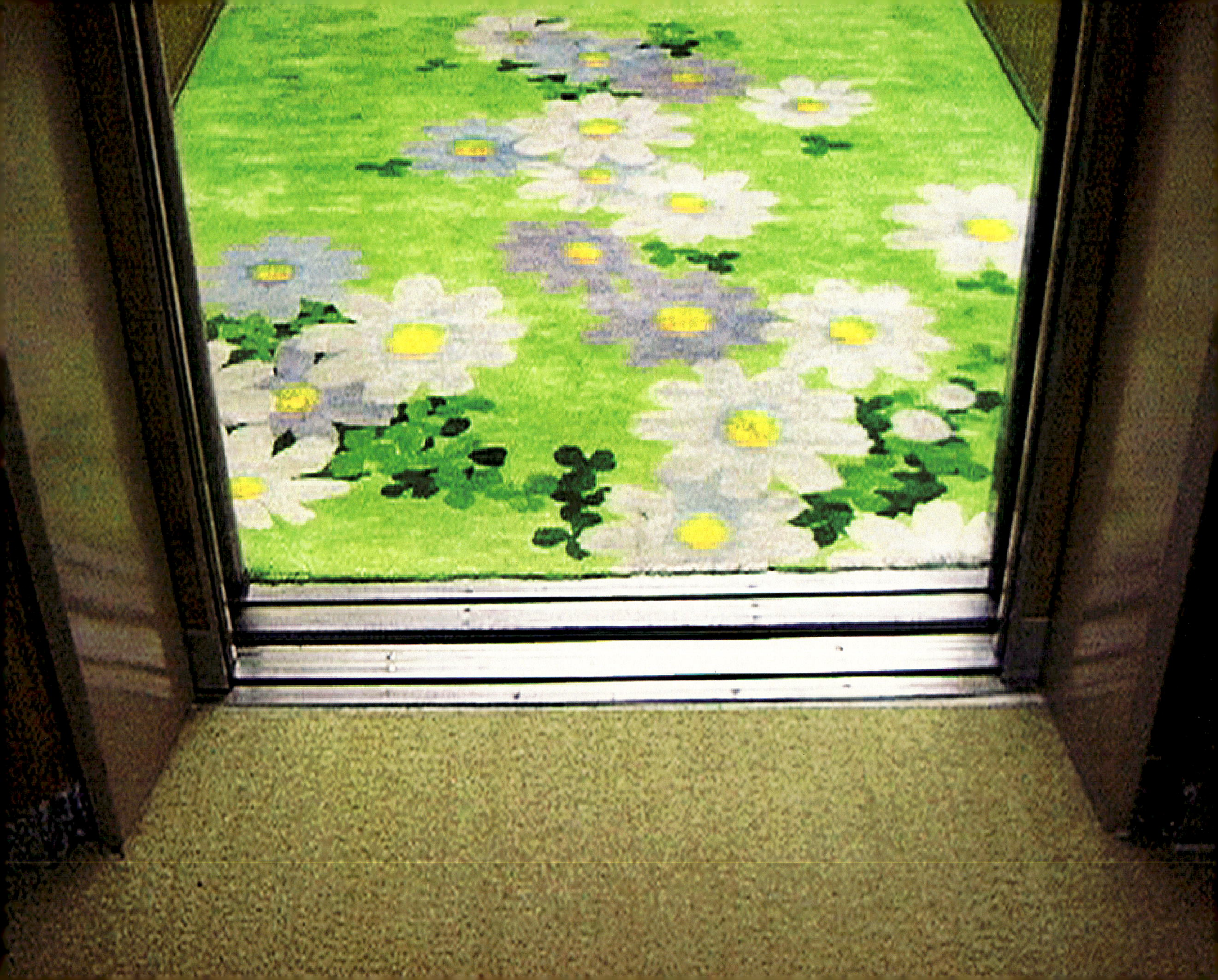

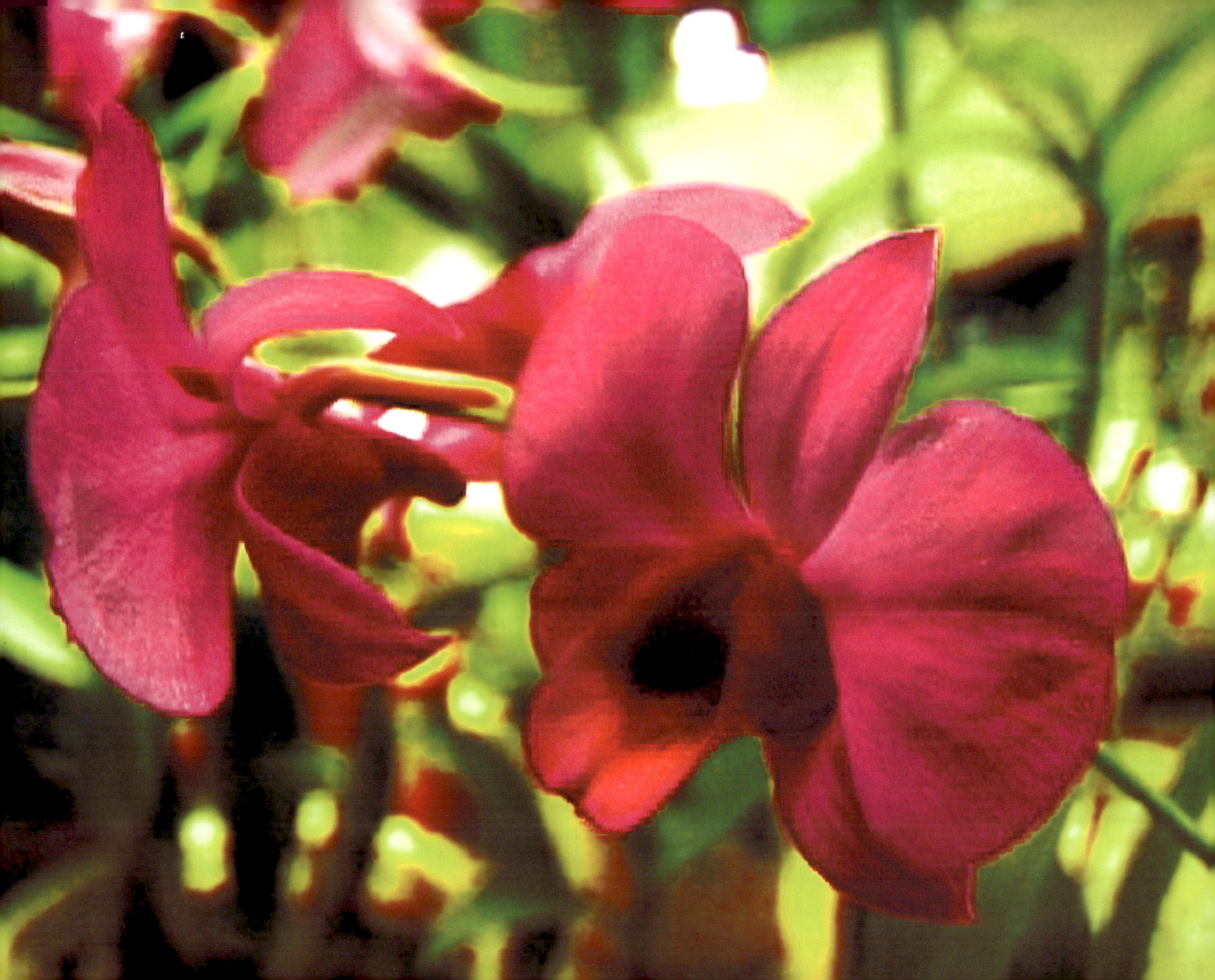

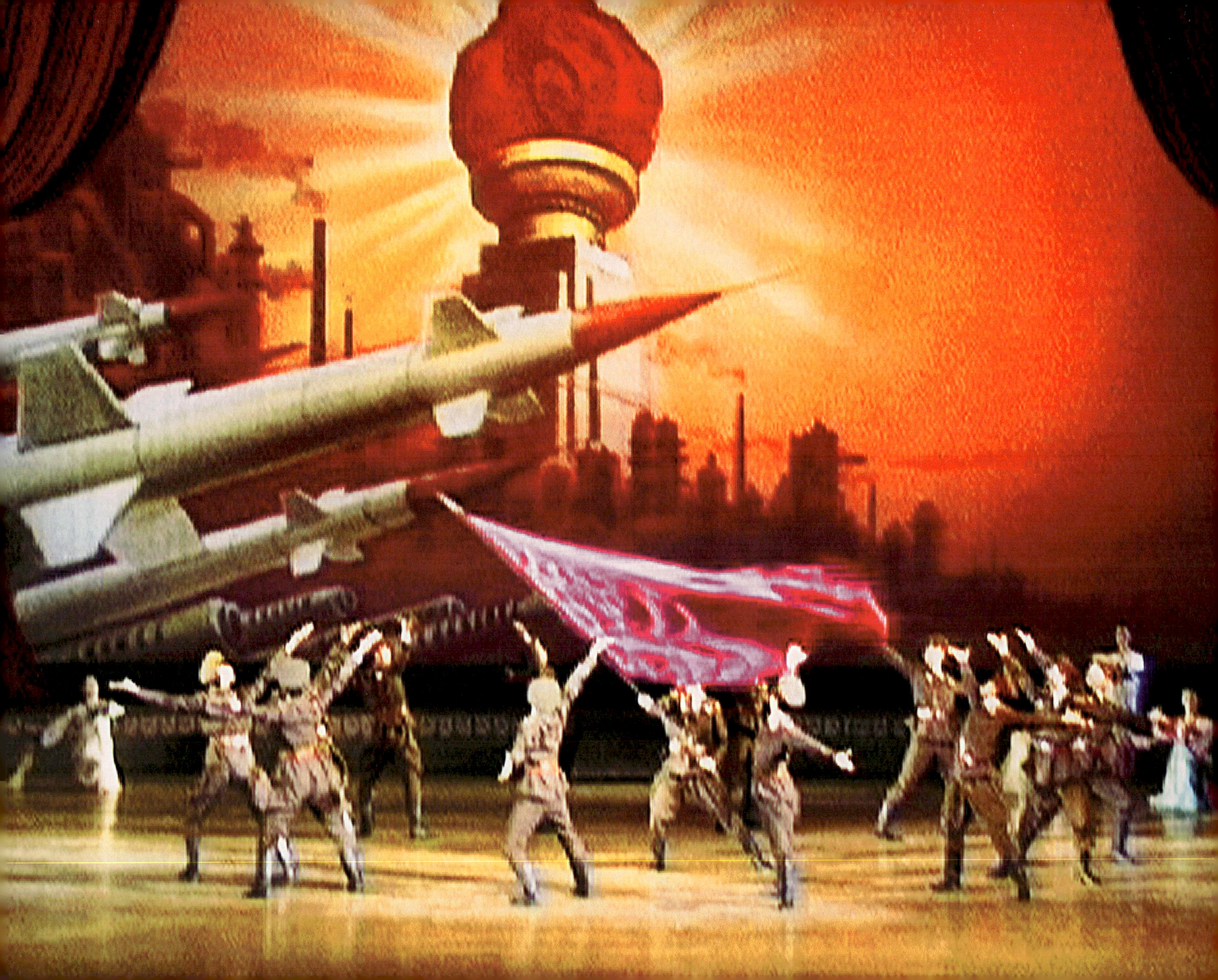

" It would be wrong to pretend that preventive strikes are an option that belongs to the U.S. alone. "

KOREAN CENTRAL NEWS AGENCY OF THE DPRK

YEAR 92 (FEBRUARY 21, 2003) **Four North Korean combat jets attempt to intimidate a U.S. spy plane flying in international airspace. Kim Jong Il threatens to withdraw from the cease-fire treaty of 1953. Pyonyang expels the inspectors of the International Nuclear Energy Agency.** YEAR 92 (JUNE 4, 2003) **The Korean Central News Agency of DPRK issues a statement declaring that "The U.S. is well advised to have a clear understanding of the DPRK's military potential and will, and to abandon its reckless attempt at preemptive nuclear attack."**

" We are happy! "

SLOGAN ON THE STREETS OF PYONGYANG

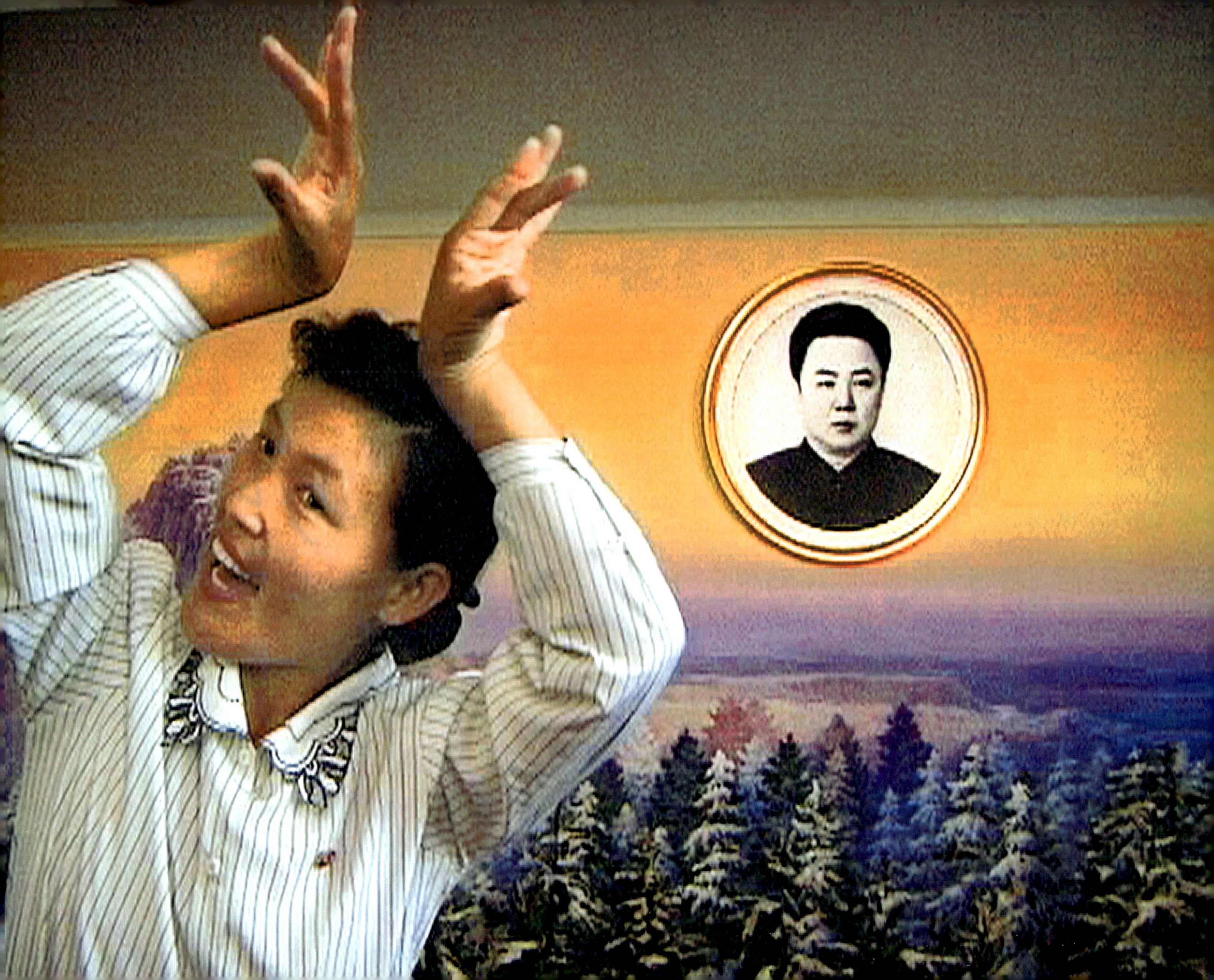

" We are happy. "

NICOLAS RIGHETTI

This is the first sentence translated for me when I arrive on the tarmac in Pyongyang, an enormous slogan written in Korean; white script on a red background. I am happy too. I feel moved to be here, to have finally managed to set foot into one of the most reclusive states in the world. It has only taken nine years of maneuvering to get a visa and four invitations extended through official channels. Four trips there and back, each proving to be more alike each time, yet somehow never ceasing to astound.

Leaving the airport, the world turns upside down. No advertisements, no traffic, no salesmen, no noise, no bicycles, no animals, no Asia as we know it. The country exists in a vacuum, cut off from the rest of the world; the atmosphere feels like that of a besieged citadel. On the road leading out of the capital city, streams of silent pedestrians in uniform walk by the hundreds down the avenues. Soldiers stand guard in full Robocop gear, ready to intervene at a moment's notice against the imperialist peril.

Han, my official guide, is on hand to show me around. Each visit, Han and I are sincerely happy to see one another again. He is convinced of my unconditional love for the regime, and I am delighted to be able to feast on the propaganda with my camera. He hands me the same program and the same schedule for my stay. The itinerary is always the same. The first time this happens, I am nonplussed, and point this out to him. "Yes, it's true, but people rarely come back!" he explains, slightly surprised by my comment. The daily visits are recorded hour by hour. Every foreign delegation welcomed to this earthly paradise is in the same boat, and even all by myself, I amount to a foreign delegation of one. My program is so full that it is impossible for me to escape from it. I am implacably constrained to stick to this rigid yet glossy itinerary: the birthplace of Kim Il Sung, the Triumphal Arch, the Museum of International Friendship, the Number One Shop, the tower representing the Juche ideology, the Children's Palace. This capital city is a huge communist version of Hollywood. There is no power without mise-en-scéne. Similar attractions produce similar emotions. The different scenes flit by as I travel through the city by bus. Inside or outside, everything seems artificial to me.

On my second excursion, I realize that what is interesting to me is not to uncover the nasty underside of this totalitarian production, but to portray the country as it wishes to appear. I decide to film the artificial happiness of the ceremonies to which I am invited, the lurid interiors, the ubiquitous smiling faces painted everywhere. Like Alice in Wonderland, I finally find myself on the other side of the mirror. I make fiction into reality—unless the opposite is true and it is reality that has turned into fiction.

All this fills me with unexpected joy—the pleasure of discovering a simple, clean, and perfect world. The great strength of the North Korean visual universe is its uniformity, homogeneity, and repetitiveness. From the slogans: "I love Comrade Kim Jong Il, the strongest man in the world," or, "Think, speak, and act like Kim Il Sung and Kim Jong Il, our dear, beloved leaders," to the official portraits decorating every apartment, state building, and dining room—all are indeed very real. See and be seen is the purpose of these twin portraits that occupy a place of honor in every household, like a placid Big Brother. The people are also supposed to wear a badge representing their leaders. Nobody can escape from the sight of power. I feel as if I have become a child in the Garden of Eden and the Father is my guide. Even in death, "Kim Il Sung still lives among us." Kim Il Sung is everywhere. He is God. His son Kim Jong Il is the Messiah and Pyongyang his earthly paradise. He has become a sacred political figure: "Comrade Kim is not only the Korean people's political protector, but also their physical savior. His love cures the sick." Kim Il Sung's omnipresence and omnipotence is visible on posters and streamers, and in books and magazines, on television or on the radio. These two patriarchal figures often appear side by side. Depicted at the same age, they seem to be atemporal and interchangeable, becoming one and the same divine icon. Faced with their image, I cannot tell whether it is I who contemplates them or they who are looking at me.

In the bus, Han describes each building tirelessly. First the Museum of the Foundation of the Party, then the bronze statue of Chollima, a winged horse signifying the "breathless speed of socialist construction and revolutionary spirit of Korea." Elsewhere, the War Museum, also known as "Victorious Fatherland Liberation War Museum," features an exhibit on the unforgettable feats of Comrade Kim Il Sung: "This great leader who, for his homeland and for his people, stopped the invasion of imperialistic allied forces." Han always has a ready answer to my questions.

When we arrive in the capital city of the People's Democratic Republic of Korea, Han translates yet another placard: "This is paradise." In fact, Pyongyang means "pleasant place" in Korean. Shops and subway stops are also baptized "paradise." For the regime, this town is the perfect archetype of the Juche paradise. What remains is to duplicate and inject it throughout the country. The "farmer comrades" have the duty to work hard in order to transplant the ideology into each community. In turn, the residents of the capital city are supposed to support the peasants when "difficulties" arise, such as famine and floods.

The streets are clean. The population is highly disciplined. Children in uniform "naturally" walk in single file to get on the school bus. The people are both the spectators and the actors of this propaganda. They act and contemplate, but only the Leaders have the power to change the staging of this artificial world. And because we are in heaven, celebrations are held one after another. The public is always present in large numbers to applaud mechanically.

There is always the contradictory feeling of emptiness and fullness. From one moment to the next, a deserted avenue suddenly fills with a crowd of youngsters. The choreography that enacts and invokes the glory of the regime can begin: two-hundred pairs of red pants and matching tee-shirts dance and sing the praise of Kim Jung Il. Cheerleaders brandish red flags. At once, they all leave as swiftly as they arrived. The city square returns to reality, empty and silent.

"Long live peace in the world," my guide declares apropos nothing in particular. A very touching man, but I can feel that anything that might disturb this wonderful balance worries him. He wants to convince me of the superiority of Korean-style communism. This sudden outburst of absurd slogans in the middle of ordinary conversations is quite common. I am getting used to it. Apart from my guide, in the street nobody speaks to me. When I am alone, no one establishes contact; no one seems to pay any attention to me. Life goes on as if I did not exist. Not even the police or soldiers take the risk of approaching me. Fear imbues us all.

If it were not for this overwhelming sense of fear, and growing awareness of the façade, I am almost ready to believe. It might have taken several return trips to this earthly paradise to realize that all this was real; that everything that is fake can also be real.

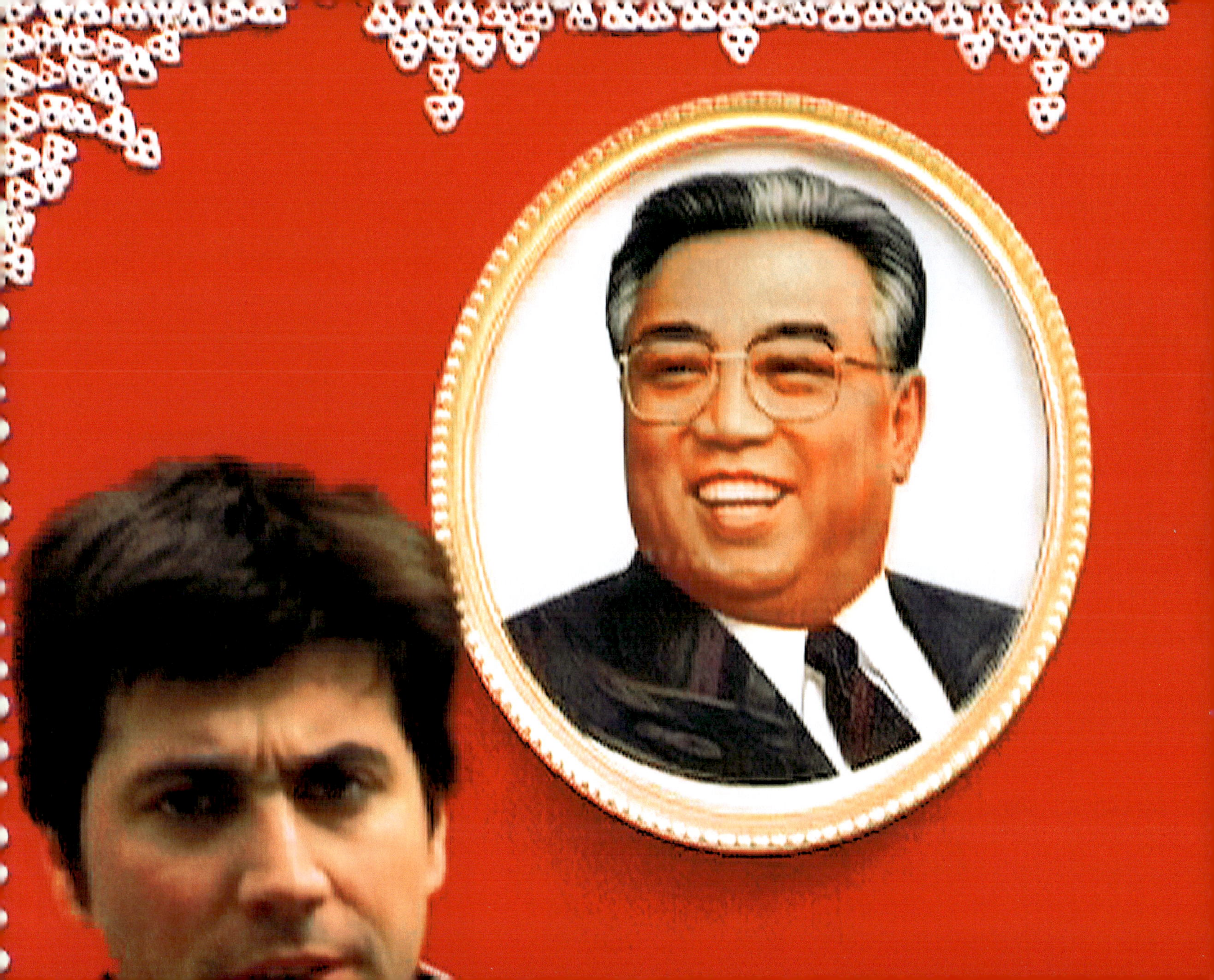

The Kimilsongism

CHEONG SEONG CHANG

According to Kim Jong Il, Juche ideology is based on the philosophical principle whereby man is master of everything. In more concrete terms, this principle infers that man is master of the world and his own destiny and therefore plays a crucial role in changing the world and shaping his future. In the Juche philosophy, "man" does not mean the individual but identifies the masses. The Juche ideology cannot be equated with western-style individualism or liberalism. It is closer to Stalin's ideology, which claims to be the working classes' ideology while justifying the personal dictatorship of the Party's socio-historical principles.

Juche ideology resembles the historical materialism of Stalin's Marxism-Leninism. These principles are as follows: it is the masses who make history in any society; the history of mankind is the history of the masses fighting for "Chajusông" (sovereignty); the socio-historical movement is the concrete expression of the masses' creativity; and lastly, due to the independent nature of their ideological awareness, the masses necessarily play a crucial role in the revolutionary struggle.

Kim Jong Il thereby converts the working masses into an "unlimited" supply of strength and intelligence. However, exalting the masses in this manner necessarily implies an authoritarian regime. He continues his line of argument adding that a genuine revolutionary struggle can only take place under the Party's sound guidance and that of the Leader. Thus, the message is clear: the masses must obey the Party, and the Party must obey the Leader. This "revolutionary concept of the Leader," which justifies his personal dictatorship, is the cornerstone of the Juche theory.

Kim Jong Il indicates that establishing Juche as an integral part of the governing ideology necessarily implies that "each individual shall acquire a point of view and attitude that obliges him to play an active role in the revolution and the edification of socialism," making him focus all his thoughts and actions on the revolution in his country and on solving any problems by applying his own intelligence and using his own strengths. This is only possible if each individual is fully acquainted with the revolutionary ideas of the working classes as well as those of the Party line and politics. At the root of the struggle to boost national pride and revolutionary zeal is the "revolutionary conception of the great Leader" and the Party's policy based on Kim Il Sung's personality cult. Establishing Juche ideology necessarily implies developing a "Juchean culture, national in form and revolutionary and socialist in substance ... which raises the standard of culture and mass techniques, as well as eliminating anything which might resemble subservience to world powers."

In North Korea, politics are defined as a "social function which organises and manages men's activities on the basis of common interests shared between certain classes or the whole of society." Political independence can only be guaranteed by grouping the people closely around the Party and its Leader. In this way, it is united under a single political force through which the Party and the people can give expression to their "immense" power. While Lenin only imposed unified action on Party members, Pyongyang's political leaders expect this discipline from the whole of society. The leaders concentrate all their efforts on "changing the whole of society by instilling the Juche philosophy." Here, communist totalitarianism reaches a degree unknown to the Soviet Union. In Kim Jong Il's eyes, the country's political independence identifies completely with political freedom of individuals.

Kim Jong Il asserts as fact that independence presupposes self-sufficiency, hence the need to build an economy which relies on its own natural resources and the power of the people, rather than depending on a foreign country. This implies an industry which can export if it overproduces, but must only import the minimum. It is also a question of "simultaneously developing heavy industry, light industry and agriculture, giving priority to the former."

Political self-defense in North Korea is provided

by the army, ostensibly backed by the people. According to the State, it has four main goals: modernizing the army, transforming the latter into an army of officers, arming all the people and establishing self-defense systems throughout the country. This policy can only be appreciated in terms of the negative impact the Korean War (1950–1953) had on the regime. Military-type discipline was henceforth imposed on the whole of the population, and the slightest criticism of the Party was severely repressed.

When Kim Jong Il speaks about the "guide who governs the way in which Juche is established," not only in respect to the activities of the Party and the State, but also in respect to other aspects of the revolution, he is referring to the three following leading principles of the Juche ideology:

IT IS ESSENTIAL TO PROTECT SOVEREIGNTY. Every citizen, sufficiently aware of the specificity of his country, must feel invested with "immense national pride" and "revolutionary zeal." All North Koreans who adhere to Juche ideology will learn more about the country's history, geography, economy, and culture, as well as "the traditions and revolutionary history of the Workers' Party.... As for North Korean communists, their job is to make sure that the whole of the population feels great pride in belonging to the brave, intelligent Korean nation, and in supporting the revolution under the guidance of the Great Leader." In other words, all North Koreans have a duty to defend national sovereignty with their lives.

A CREATIVE ATTITUDE SHOULD BE ADOPTED IN TERMS OF WORKING METHODS. This second leading principle includes the two following elements: searching for support from the masses and taking concrete reality into account. Regarding the first method, Kim Jong Il maintains that the masses know what reality means better than anyone else. However, he believes that only by "synthesizing and generalizing" the people's opinions and demands, is it possible to establish a trend keeping with the public's aspirations and interests. Therefore, it is not the masses, but the Party, and hence the Leader, who decides which of the regime's basic operations should be carried out by the whole of the society. The method, referred to as the "Great Leader's working method" consists in constantly mixing with the masses in order to be fully acquainted with concrete reality and to find the most effective and creative means of problem solving. This method gives more weight to political matters than any other activities, encouraging the masses to use "their own willpower to accomplish their allotted tasks." Kim Jong Il asserts that the country's political independence is directly in line with the political freedom of individuals.

THE IMPORTANCE OF IDEOLOGY SHOULD BE EMPHASIZED. Today, the North Korean regime considers its main task is to convert man into a Juchean Communist. This "reborn communist" is defined as an "ever-faithful follower of the Party and the Leader even at the risk of his own life." In the People's Democratic Republic of Korea, the main purpose of the "Reborn Communist" project, representing a new totalitarian political culture, is to justify the Party's power.

In the name of this revolution, North Korean communists attach great importance to "revolutionary study." According to the Beloved Leader Kim Jong Il, a supporter of the revolution must always consider study to be of prime importance and devote the whole of his life to it. Workers are therefore encouraged to spend thirty minutes of their time reading when they arrive at work every morning. In this way, they read about Juche and other documents, such as the "Memoirs" of the war veterans of the anti-Japanese armed combat. Furthermore, all teenagers and adults must know Kim Il Sung's and Kim Jong Il's revolutionary texts by heart.

To conclude, Juche ideology, initially designed to establish Kim Il Sung's power and eliminate his opponents, continues to reinforce a centralized power on a lasting basis, justifying the ongoing personality cult of the leader, leaving the door open to any type of extreme political, economic, and cultural views.

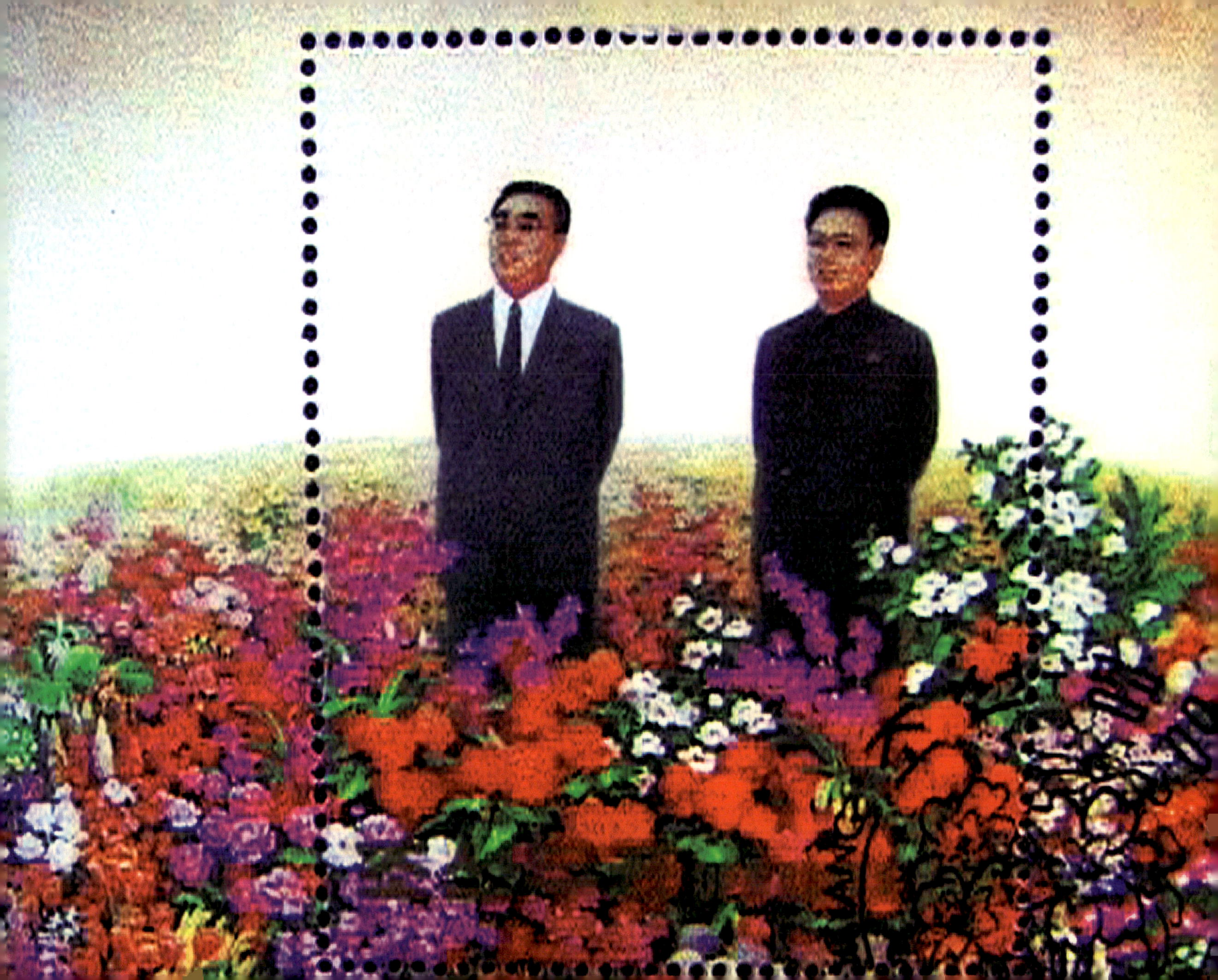

NICOLAS RIGHETTI was born in Geneva, Switzerland, where he studied at the Institut d'Etudes Sociales and the Ecole Suprérieure d'Audio Visuel. Righetti has traveled, photographed, and filmed extensively throughout Asia, working as a still photographer on the set of various feature films in Hong Kong, Beijing, and Paris. His photographs have appeared in numerous publications worldwide.

ORVILLE SCHELL is one of the world's foremost experts on Asia. Now Dean of the University of California Berkeley Graduate School of Journalism, his groundbreaking work includes the 1995 *Mandate of Heaven* (one of fourteen published works to date), and frequent writing for the *New Yorker*, *Harpers*, *Newsweek*, *Atlantic Monthly*, and *The New York Times Magazine*. His work as a network correspondent (ABC, CBS, NBC, CNN) also underlines his stature as a leading journalist on Asia.

CHEONG SEONG CHANG studied political science at Kyunghee University in Seoul before moving to France to pursue and continue his research on the North Korean regime. He has already published in his country several articles on the topic of the Korean reunification, and a book entitled *Politiques des deux Corées et tâches des mouvements sud-coréens pour la réunification* (Politics of the two Koreas and South Korea's tasks in the movement for reunification).

The following were used in research and selecting excerpts for inclusion in this book:

BONG, BAIK. *Kim Il Sung Biographie 1.* Beyrouth: Dar Al-Talia, 1973.

CHOL-HWAN, KANG. *Les Aquariums de Pyongang: dix ans de goulag nord-coréen.* Paris: Robert Laffont, 2000.

DESTEXHE, ALAIN. *Corée du Nord: Voyage en Dynastie Totalitaire.* Paris: Harmattan, 2001.

EBERSTADT, NICOLAS. *The End of North Korea.* Washington: AEI Press, 1999.

GRANGEREAU, PHILLIPPE. *Au Pays du Grand Mensonge: Voyage en Corée du Nord.* Paris: Serpent de Mer, 2001.

HA, KIM TCHANG. *Les Immortelles: Idees du Djoutche.* Pyongang, 1984.

IL, KIM ET TCHOÉ HYEUN. *Vingt Années de la Revolution Antijaponaise sous le Soleil Rouge.* Pyongyang, 1981.

OBERDORFER, DAN. *The Two Koreas: A Contemporary History.* Cambridge, MA: Perseus Publishing, 1997.

RIGOULOT, PIERRE. *Corée du Nord, État voyou,* Paris: Buchet-Chastel, 2003.

SEONG-CHANG, CHENONG. *Ideologie et Systheme en Corée du Nord.* Paris: Harmattan, 1997.

SOCIÉTÉ D'EXPORTATION ET D'IMPORTATION DES FILMS. *Un Grand Homme et le Film.* Pyongyang,1998.

TAKASHI, NADA. *Kim Jong Il et Son Peuple.* Pyongyang, 1984.

Other sources include: *Rodong Shinmun*, the daily official paper of the North Korean Worker's Party; Radio Pyongyang; the archives of the author and chronology created by the AFP (Associated French Press); and the Korea News Service (Tokyo).

Some selections were gathered from the French-language publication, *Editions en Langues Etrangères*, issued from Pyongyang on a monthly basis, including the following volumes: 1980, *Le soleil genereux*; 1986, KIM JONG IL *la vie et la literature*; 1987, KIM JONG IL *les personnages et les acteurs*; 1989, KIM JONG IL *une grande personnalité*; 1982, KIM IL SUNG *à propos du Djoutche dans notre révolution (numéro3)*; 1982, KIM IL SUNG *sur les trois principes de la réunification de la patrie;* 1989, KIM JONG IL, *De L'art Cinematographique*; 1992, KIM JONG IL *oeuvres choisies*; 1993, KIM IL SUNG *grand homme de notre siècle*; 1995, PYONGYANG *apercu general*; 1997, KIM IL SUNG *ouvre (numéro 42)*; 1998, KIM JONG IL *le socialisme est une science.*

The Last Paradise

First Edition
English language HC ISBN 1-884167-32-2

Umbrage Editions, Inc.
515 Canal Street
New York, New York, 10013
www.umbragebooks.com

Publisher: Nan Richardson
Editor: Lesley A. Martin
Exhibitions Coordinator: Launa Beuhler
Assistant Editors: Raya Kuzyk, Emily Baker
Editorial Assistants: Andrea Dunlap, Sarina Finkelstein, Sarah P. Hanson, Nathan Heiges, Jon Lesser, Hank W. Lee, Justin Meade, Jaime Schwartz

www.umbragebooks.com

Designed by Alain Robert Studio
www.alain-robert.ch

Photolithos by Imagie
www. imagie.com

Printed in Italy by Artegrafica Srl, Verona, Italy